8.95

The Feast of Faith

JOSEPH CARDINAL RATZINGER

The Feast of Faith

Approaches to a Theology of the Liturgy

Translated by Graham Harrison

IGNATIUS PRESS   SAN FRANCISCO

Title of the German original:
Das Fest des Glaubens
© 1981 Johannes Verlag
Einsiedeln, Switzerland

Cover by Victoria Hoke Lane

With ecclesiastical approval
© 1986 Ignatius Press, San Francisco
ISBN 0-89870-056-6
Library of Congress catalogue number 85-82175
Printed in the United States of America

Contents

Preface

Faced with the political and social crises of the present time and the moral challenge they offer to Christians, the problems of liturgy and prayer could easily seem to be of second importance. But the question of the moral standards and spiritual resources that we need if we are to acquit ourselves in this situation cannot be separated from the question of worship. Only if man, every man, stands before the face of God and is answerable to him, can man be secure in his dignity as a human being. Concern for the proper form of worship, therefore, is not peripheral but central to our concern for man himself.

So it seemed worthwhile to present for publication a collection of pieces on the question of Christian liturgy. They arose in part from the needs of my official ministry and in part from the reflection which is inseparable from it. All the chapters were revised and reedited for this publication. They can be no more than fragments, characterized and no doubt limited by the particular contemporary situation; yet perhaps for that very reason they may help others to come to grips with today's issues. All that is written here is governed by the one fundamental question, namely, how, under modern conditions, we can pray and join in the Church's praise of God, and how we can see and experience the salvation of man and the glory of God as a single whole.

Joseph Cardinal Ratzinger
Munich, Ash Wednesday, 1981

Part One

Basic Considerations
In a Theology of Liturgy

On the Theological Basis
Of Prayer and Liturgy

I. The End of Religion?

1. A contemporary dispute

A few years ago those interested in the debate about Christianity could have followed a characteristically confusing dispute which appeared in the *Süddeutsche Zeitung*.[1] The Dominican Father Anselm Hertz published an article entitled "Have We Come to the End of All Religion?", in which he presented a totally irresponsible picture of the course of history, albeit one that has gained wide currency. In former times, so he maintained, religion had been the public and private bond linking society and the individual to God or the gods; it was manifest in pious conduct and in cultic behavior. No doubt as a rhetorical ploy, he illustrates his argument (with references to Augustine) by citing the prayer made by both sides in war for victory or preservation. (Thus the reader is encouraged to associate the issue of prayer with that of war.) His supposedly logical conclusion with regard to the phenomenon of war is evidently meant to be of general application: "The metaphysical, transcendental reference of all causes has been dismantled; and if the cause can no longer be interpreted metaphysically, a

---

[1] Published as N. Lobkowicz and A. Hertz, *Am Ende aller Religion? Ein Streitgespräch* (Zurich 1976).

metaphysical view of the effects becomes superfluous too."[2] This general proposition is then reapplied to the concrete case, yielding the characteristic aside: "Prayer for victory or preservation in battle has become meaningless, even if now and then armies and weapons continue to be blessed."[3]

According to Fr. Hertz's scheme of history, private piety was able to keep going for a long time after the demise of public religion. God was no longer responsible "for the events of war as a whole but only for the fate of his faithful ones". It is thus an easy matter to describe this phase of religious history as schizophrenia and go on to make the reader aware that the time for private piety, too, has run out.[4] At this point he goes beyond the topic of war which up to now provided the argument: a God who "was primarily seen as a God of the weather, of protection and blessing" has disappeared, and this means that a God of transcendence, standing over against immanence, belongs "to the magical and mythical substrata of human religiosity" which has been "nowadays largely overcome".[5] Now the new form of religion heaves in sight, the third phase of this view of history, in which modern man is ensconced, finally, above all the errors and false starts of the past: now the criterion of religion is no longer "in what forms man's attachment to God is expressed, but whether man is ready and able to transcend himself".[6] No doubt all men may aspire to this

[2] Ibid., 21.

[3] Ibid.

[4] Ibid.

[5] Ibid., 26.

[6] Ibid., 27. Characteristic is the following: "Not only has God many names; there is also a wealth of possibilities of communication with him. Perhaps this is something we have yet to learn if we are to

readiness, this capacity, especially as what it implies is left totally vague.

However, while the good Dominican was endeavoring to console the reader for the loss of a personal God (albeit by too obvious a sleight-of-hand in the matter of prayer in time of war), the political theorist Lobkowicz was pulling the veil from his somewhat confused arguments. Not mincing matters, he simply asked what this "self-transcendence" meant: "What good is it for Hertz to urge us to transcend ourselves? A propos, it is noticeably those who think they are too superior to talk simply and concretely of God who are in the habit of talking about 'transcendence'. . . . Suppose I had achieved this transcendence and come face to face with the 'ultimate ground of being' which 'is manifest everywhere in the world, wherever man is searching for the abiding meaning of his existence'. What then? Do I respectfully salute this 'ground of being' and simply return to the hardness of my daily life?—or does this encounter become a fundamental experience causing me to see everything differently and revolutionizing my behavior?"[7] With refreshing clarity Lobkowicz has expressed the fact that "every theology which no longer facilitates petitionary prayer, and hence thanksgiving, is a fraud."[8]

---

realize that, in spite of the decline of the traditional religions, we are nearer to God than we think."

[7] Ibid., 34.

[8] Ibid., 17. It must be mentioned here that, at the conclusion of the debate, Hertz seems to make large concessions to Lobkowicz, most noticeably when he says: "I do believe that this God whom Jesus proclaimed, who bears good will to all men, can be our partner in prayer when we speak to him of our joys, sorrows and anxieties. This is no mythical God but the God who reveals himself in Jesus Christ. . . ." However, this does not square with the overall impression he gives, where the received Christian faith is completely

This drama, in which theology keeps talking although
the God who can speak and listen has long ago submerged
together with the myths, is fascinating in the way it
seems to spread, presenting itself quietly, piously, without the least trumpeting of heresy, as the most natural
thing in the world. It is impossible to read without deep
sadness the "prayer", expressive of this approach, with
which G. Hasenhüttl concludes his "Introduction to the
Doctrine of God"—a prayer which no longer addresses
anyone, desperately trying to convince itself that man
still has access to meaning and love and that the experience
of this is "God" for man. Let us read a little of it to see
what "transcendence" means in this kind of theology—a
somber dialogue with the void, trying to keep up its
courage and calling itself "prayer":

> It was easy to pray when in simplicity of heart I could still
> kneel down and know that there was a God in heaven to
> see me. I could lay my anxieties and joys before him and
> know that he heard me, even if I could not always
> experience that he did.
>   Today I am part of a social order in which the relation
> of lord to servant has finally been abolished, and this

---

absorbed into the general history of religion, causing Lobkowicz
rightly to comment on Hertz's initial explanations: "In the same
breath you speak of the Christian faith in God, the Greek oracles and
the Etruscan divination practice of inspecting entrails" (61). Even in
the conciliatory conclusion, however, the personal God disappears
into the mist—and throughout the discussion he had never achieved
the status of a God who acts—when Hertz says: "Is it not enough to
believe that in and through Jesus Christ the 'Kingdom of God' has
come to us and that we men are called to collaborate in bringing about
this kingdom of peace and love? God wills the salvation of all men,
and in his kindness he will bring to a happy conclusion the good he
has begun in us" (84). In plain language this means that it is up to us to
work for a better future; God is allotted a modest place in it insofar as
he will eventually take a hand too.

means that I can no longer feel that God is Lord and I am his unworthy servant. It would be meaningless now to fall down in worship with eyes full of tears of joy or sorrow. It is hard now to address God as "Thou", for the only "Thou" I know is the human "Thou", in all its ambivalence. I am a partner to my fellow men in society, but God is not my partner. . . .

So I know, here and now, stripped of all illusions, that I am affirmed, that there is meaning in the absurdity of life, a meaning which brings happiness. I am affirmed every time I give love, when I collaborate in the making of the society of the future, for all its provisional character. So, even today, I can cry out like the psalmist thousands of years ago and say: Yes, he is; I am affirmed; God is! And if you want to dispense with the word "God", well and good, but keep its place open, for the reality it signifies will come to you, will force you to decide, and in love it will be revealed to you and you will find yourself crying out: "Yes, do you see? God is when men love one another!"

It often happens nowadays that we can no longer call upon God because he is not the powerful Lord; similarly we cannot live in hope of a paradisal future since it is only a creation of man's imagination. But we can thank and pray, knowing, in all our brokenness, that today itself gives us hope for the future; we live today believing in new possibilities; today we can love, we will love, for it is only today that we can experience God, it is only today that he is near to us.[9]

---

[9] G. Hasenhüttl, *Einführung in die Gotteslehre* (Darmstadt 1980), 242f. For a systematic presentation of the underlying rationale, cf. G. Hasenhüttl, *Kritische Dogmatik* (Graz 1979). A central axiom of the *Gotteslehre*: "God is a predicate of man, says something about man in the area of relational communication" (132). For a detailed analysis of Hasenhüttl's position, cf. F. Courth, "Nur ein anderer Weg der Dogmatik? Zu G. Hasenhüttls kritischer Dogmatik" in *TThZ* 89 (1980): 293–317. Cf. also the reviews of P. Hünermann, in *Theol. Revue* 76 (1980): 212–25 (with a response from Hasenhüttl, 409f.);

2. Where does the Bible stand?

We do not know what human experiences, sufferings and crises lie behind words such as these; we must respect them: it is not our business to judge. On the other hand, we are obliged to state firmly that this is not Christian theology. For the prime characteristic of Christian faith is that it is faith in God. Furthermore, that this God is someone who speaks, someone to whom man can speak. The Christian God is characterized by revelation, that is, by the words and deeds in which he addresses man, and the goal of revelation is man's response in word and deed, which thus expands revelation into a dialogue between Creator and creature which guides man toward union with God.[10] So prayer is not something on the periphery of the Christian concept of God; it is a fundamental trait. The whole Bible is dialogue: on the one side, revelation, God's words and deeds, and on the other side, man's response in accepting the word of God and allowing himself to be led by God. To delete prayer and dialogue, genuine two-way dialogue, is to delete the whole Bible.

We must insist, however, that the Bible in no way needs to be "rescued" from a mythical world view

---

W. Beinert in *Theol. prakt. Quartalschr.* 128 (1980): 304; W. Löser, in *Theol. Phil.* 55 (1980): 616f.

[10] Thus it is one of Hertz's false alternatives (op. cit. 26f.) when he gives the impression that one must either maintain an unbridgeable gulf between transcendence and immanence or consign both of them to a philosophy of "transcendence". In fact, as we can see clearly in the case of Jaspers, "transcendence" thus becomes totally inaccessible, whereas an understanding of God which includes creation and revelation involves the reciprocal relationship and union of "immanence" and "transcendence".

which supposedly encapsulates it; it does not need to be "helped" on the way towards its fuller development. The reverse is the case: Greek philosophy had come to the conclusion that it was impossible to pray to God, since the Eternal One, by being eternal, cannot enter into time relations. This led to such an utter separation of philosophy and religion, of reason and piety, that it heralded the end of ancient religion. Later indeed it did try to rescue the old religions by acknowledging in them a demythologized meaning, in the way many theologians today try to demythologize dogma and sacrament. We can see in this endeavor the last traces of nostalgia for the lost world of the religions—the attempt to save what has been lost, even if its original meaning can no longer be entertained. This romantic reaction may have been able to slow down the decline of the gods, but it could not stop it. It simply lacked truth.

In this process, which involved all the questions raised in the current debate, the Christian faith took up a unique position. With regard to the concept of God, it held to the enlightened view of the philosophers: the gods are illusory; they do not exist. What Christians call "God" is what the philosophers call "being", "ground" or (also) "God". They are not afraid to say that it is this God of the philosophers who is their God too. What is unique about their position is that they attribute to the God of the philosophers the fundamental trait of the gods of the old religions, namely, the relationship with men, albeit now in an absolute form insofar as they call God the Creator. This paradoxical conjunction consti-tutes the Christian synthesis, its outstanding novelty; it is the source of the basic difficulty and vulnerability of the Christian position in the history of religions: only

"The Absolute" can be God, but this very Absolute has the attribute of being "relative", relationship, Creator and Revealer, or as later tradition would put it, "Person", someone who addresses the creature and to whom the creature can turn. This synthesis also distinguishes the Christian faith from the "mythical" religions like those of Asia and connects it with Judaism and Islam, although Christianity exhibits a unique and distinct form in its belief in the Trinity. Ultimately all questions come back to the enormous tension created by *this* synthesis; the modern situation has not really introduced anything radically new. In the end, of course, whether this synthesis can be affirmed depends, not on philosophical considerations, but on whether one has been given the degree of spiritual tension which corresponds to the tension of the Christian idea of God.[11]

3. Arguments against prayer

Consequently, in our efforts to work out the theological and anthropological basis of prayer, it is not a question of proving the validity of Christian prayer by the standards of some neutral reasonableness. It is a case of uncovering the inner logic of faith itself, with its own distinct reasonableness. Our first step, however, must be to ask briefly what are the substantial reasons which seem to militate against prayer's reasonableness. I observe three kinds, occurring naturally in countless variations and combinations.

[11] In connection with these remarks on the ancient world's notion of God, cf. my own *Volk und Haus Gottes in Augustins Lehre von der Kirche* (Munich 1954); also in brief my *Introduction to Christianity* (London 1969, New York 1979), 94–104.

a. Firstly there is the general rejection of a metaphysical way of approach, corresponding to the main thrust of contemporary thought. Karl Jaspers has clothed this rejection in a religious form in his philosophy; his explicit aim is to continue religion without metaphysics, or rather to see the farewell to metaphysics as a better way of legitimizing faith and spirituality. From what we have said so far it should be clear that the results of this approach are in fact very different from what is envisaged by the Bible and the faith of the Church. For Christian faith it is essential that it is addressing the God who really exists, the Creator of all things and the ground of all being, and that this God has spoken to us. To reject metaphysics is to reject creation and hence the Christian concept of God itself. Conversely, now as always, it is the belief in creation which is the strongest rational foundation for the Christian idea of God and its metaphysical implications, as is very clear from J. Monod's consistent line of thought.[12]

---

[12] J. Monod, *Zufall und Notwendigkeit. Philosophische Fragen der modernen Biologie* (Munich 1971). In its consistent thought this book seems to me to be one of the most important works contributing to a deeper dialogue between science and theology. It carefully presents the current state of scientific knowledge and conscientiously uncovers the philosophical presuppositions and, in doing so, gets beyond the usual blurring of issues. Cf. the foolish and wrongheaded approach of A. Dumas and O. H. Pesch on "creation", in J. Feiner and L. Vischer, *Neues Glaubensbuch* (Freiburg 1973), 430–39. Here they say that "concepts like selection and mutation are intellectually more honest than that of creation" (433). "Creation is thus an unreal concept" (435). "Creation refers to man's vocation" (435). Corresponding to this reinterpretation of the concept of creation, the teaching on faith lacks any element of belief in creation; the pages referred to come from the chapter on "History and Cosmos", included in the area of

b. Even if metaphysical questions are not rejected in principle, there is a second objection to a God of revelation. This was already formulated in the philosophy of the ancients, but it has acquired far greater force in the modern scientific and technological world. It can be put like this: a rationally constructed world is determined by rationally perceived causality. To such a scheme the notion of personal intervention is both mythical and repugnant. But if this approach is adopted, it must be followed consistently, for what applies to God applies equally to man. If there is only *one* kind of causality, man too as a person is excluded and reduced to an element in mechanical causality, in the realm of necessity; freedom too, in this case, is a mythical idea. In this sense it can be said that the personalities of God and of man cannot be separated. If personality is not a possibility, i.e., not present, with the "ground" of reality, it is not possible at all. Either freedom is a possibility inherent in the ground of reality, or it does not exist. Thus the issue of prayer is intimately linked with those of freedom and personality: the question of prayer decides whether the world is to be conceived as pure "chance and necessity" or whether freedom and love are constitutive elements of it.

c. Finally, there is a real theological objection to a God who operates *ad extra* in creation and revelation. Aristotle was the first to put it in its most pointed form; it has always been behind the scenes in Christian theology, and to this day it has probably not been fully dealt with. According to this objection, eternity by its very nature

---

ethics (part 4, Faith and the World). From a historical point of view this deletion of faith in creation is gnostic, strictly speaking; cf. J. Ratzinger, *Konsequenzen des Schöpfungsglaubens* (Salzburg 1980). Cf. also the thorough treatment of the doctrine of creation in J. Auer, *Die Welt–Gottes Schöpfung* (Regensburg 1975).

cannot enter into relationship with time, and similarly time cannot affect eternity. Eternity implies immutability, the concentrated fullness of being, removed from the vicissitudes of time. Time is essentially changeable and changing. If it were to initiate anything new in eternity, eternity would have become time. And if eternity were to get involved with the changing stream of time, it would forfeit its nature as eternity. Here we cannot go into the question of whether the concept of eternity employed in these undoubtedly logical trains of thought is adequate. So far, the debate on that particular issue has not come up with any convincing results; it needs to be continued. It will be essential to probe more deeply into the concept of "relation" if progress is to be made at this point; furthermore, instead of the negative "time-lessness" of eternity, we need to work out a concept of the creativity which eternity exercises with regard to time.[13]

There is a further aspect, which brings us directly to the Christian answer. I would like to put forward this thesis: a non-trinitarian monotheism can hardly meet Aristotle's objection. In the end it will simply have to leave eternity and time as isolated opposites. But if they cannot communicate with one another, that is, if there cannot be a reciprocal influence between time and eternity, then eternity (if there is an eternity) can be of no significance to men. For it has no power in the world, no

---

[13] For a presentation of the problem (albeit not very convincing when it comes to a solution), cf. M. Maas, *Unveränderlichkeit Gottes* (Paderborn 1974). There are important clues toward a new approach in H. U. von Balthasar, *Theologie der Geschichte* (new ed. Einsiedeln 1959); id., *Das Ganze im Fragment* (Einsiedeln 1963); valuable remarks on a correct understanding of eternity in E. Brunner, *Dogmatik I* (Zurich 1953), 282–88. Cf. the book referred to in note 16 below.

influence on human life. It is this feeling which caused the monotheism underlying ancient religion to die out in favor of the idea of the *Deus otiosus*. There is such a God, people thought, but he is separated from man by an unbridgeable chasm. Since he has no power with regard to man, he cannot matter to him either. This feeling is fundamental to the separation of philosophy and religion which we have observed in ancient times. Thus in a rational world, where faith is reduced to rational monotheism, the notion of God simply fades away: it becomes irrelevant. The Enlightenment dissolved the Christian mystery and left it with an ephemeral monotheism. Deism is not a new creation of the Enlightenment: it is merely the return of the *Deus otiosus* of the mythical religions. It either invokes the old gods or heralds the total rejection of the notion of God, or at least the rejection of a praying religion and the transition to a religiously tinged "self-transcendence". This, it seems to me, is the deepest cause of the crisis in theology which we have observed in men like Hertz and Hasenhüttl. Initially what happens is that people become uncertain about the christological and trinitarian mystery; its relationship to exegesis is felt to be problematical; it is regarded as a Hellenistic scheme projected into the universe of linear time, a necessary element of its age but now no longer intelligible. But the retreat to a rationally presentable monotheism is always merely the first step. Next comes the abandonment of the relational categories of creation and revelation. Thus this God himself fades into the concept of "transcendence". The possibility of prayer being "heard" dwindles, and faith becomes "self-transcendence".

4. Life with a religious flavor but without a God who hears

Before turning to the positive side we must investigate a little more closely what kind of religion is still possible under the presupposition of a God who cannot "relate". In accord with those who follow Jaspers, we have termed such a possibility the religion of "self-transcendence". History, however, allows us to be more precise. In fact we can speak of two major basic possibilities.

a. Aristotle ascribes significance to the prayer which fails to reach God in that it "fosters what is best in us".[14] At bottom this is identical with what modern theologians mean by "self-transcendence". Karl Barth would see it as that "religion" which is the very opposite of faith. It is strange indeed: whereas two decades ago, in the enthusiasm for Bonhoeffer, people pleaded for a religion-less faith, now everything is reversed: everything now tends toward the preservation of religion and a religious flavor to life, even though its original content, faith, is represented as untenable. This pseudo-religiosity cannot be expected to last, however, all the more since its content is too unstable, following every wind of change because it is not oriented to truth, being merely a matter of "relation", addressing a something which does not reci-procate that relation. It is trying to be a *relatio pura* which no longer contains anything that can be objectified.[15] But in reality this "pure relation" is spurious: relation without reciprocity has no meaning.

b. By contrast, the path of the Asiatic religions seems

[14] Cf. the section in this book "On the Theological Basis of Church Music", note 29.

[15] As Hasenhüttl expressly says; cf. the passages mentioned by Courth, op. cit. (note 9 above), 299f.

logically consistent and religiously profound: they start from the ultimate identity of the "I", which is in reality not an "I", with the divine ground of the world. Here prayer is the discovery of this identity, in which, behind the surface illusion, I find my own, serene identity with the ground of all being and thus am liberated from the false identity of the individualized "I". Prayer is letting myself be absorbed into what I really am; it is the gradual disappearance of what, to the separate "I", seems to be the real world. It is liberation in that one bids farewell to the empirical, experienced world with its chaos of illusion and enters the pure nothingness which is truly divine.

There can be no doubt that this is a path of impressive proportions; moreover, it appeals strongly to man's painful experience, which causes him to wish to abandon what seems to be the illusory surface of being. Only a radical abandonment of being, in favor of nothingness, seems to offer hope of real freedom. It is no accident, therefore, that the way of Asia presents itself as the way of salvation wherever the content of faith is relegated to the level of an untenable piece of Western metaphysics or mythology yet where there is still a deep spiritual and religious will. I believe that as far as religion is concerned, the present age will have to decide ultimately between the Asiatic religious world view and the Christian faith. I have no doubt that both sides have a great deal to learn from each other. The issue may be which of the two can rescue more of the other's authentic content. But in spite of this possibility of mutual exchange, no one will dispute the fact that the two ways are different. In a nutshell one could say that the goal of Asiatic contemplation is the escape from personality, whereas biblical prayer is essentially a relation between persons and hence ultimately the affirmation of the person.

II. The Structure and Content of Christian Prayer

In Part Two our task is to develop the positive basis of Christian prayer. As we have already said, it is not enough to approach it with external proofs; we must attempt, at least in outline, to reveal its intrinsic logic.[16]

1. The formal structure of Christian prayer

a. The basic reason why man can speak with God arises from the fact that God himself is speech, word. His nature is to speak, to hear, to reply, as we see particularly in Johannine theology, where Son and Spirit are described in terms of pure "hearing"; they speak in response to what they have first heard. Only because there is already speech, "Logos", in God can there be speech, "Logos", to God. Philosophically we could put it like this: the Logos in God is the onto-logical foundation for prayer. The Prologue of John's Gospel speaks of this connection in its very first sentences: "In the beginning was the Word, and the Word was in communication with God" (1:1)—as a more precise translation of the Greek πρός suggests, rather than the usual "with God". It expresses the act of turning to God, of relationship. Since there is relationship within God himself, there can also be a participation in this relationship. Thus we can relate to God in a way which does not contradict his nature.

b. In God, we have said, there is speech and the intercourse of partners in dialogue. Man could speak with God if he himself were drawn to share in this

---

[16] In a publication of this kind I need not give an exhaustive list of available literature on the philosophy and theology of prayer. As an example there is the penetrating book by H. Schaller, *Das Bittgebet. Eine theologische Skizze* (Einsiedeln 1979).

internal speech. And this is what the Incarnation of the
Logos means: he who is speech, Word, Logos, in God
and to God, participates in human speech. This has a
reciprocal effect, involving man in God's own internal
speech. Or we could say that man is able to participate in
the dialogue within God himself because God has first
shared in human speech and has thus brought the two
into communication with one another. The Incarnation
of the Logos brings eternity into time and time into
eternity. It is not that God *is* time, but he *has* time.[17] As a
result of the Incarnation, human speech has become a
component in divine speech; it has been taken up,
unconfusedly and inseparably, into that speech which is
God's inner nature.

c. Through the Spirit of Christ, who is the Spirit of
God, we can share in the human nature of Jesus Christ;
and in sharing in his dialogue with God, we can share in
the dialogue which God *is*. This is prayer, which becomes
a real exchange between God and man.

d. The locus of this identification with Christ, facilitated by the Spirit, which necessarily implies that those
involved are also identified with one another in Christ, is
what we call "Church". We could in fact define "Church"
as the realm of man's discovery of his identity through
the identification with Christ which is its source.

2. The content of Christian prayer

A fundamental word in the mouth of "the Son" is
"Abba". It is no accident that we find this word charac-
terizing the figure of Jesus in the New Testament. It
expresses his whole being, and all that he says to God in

[17] Cf. H. U. von Balthasar, *Theologie der Geschichte*, 31–39.

prayer is ultimately only an explication of his being (and hence an explication of this one word); the Our Father is this same "Abba" transposed into the plural for the benefit of those who are his.

Let us try to ascertain the content, the inner intentionality, of this basic act of prayer (which is the Son's act of being, as Son, and which thus is rooted in the ultimate ontological depths of reality). First we can say that it is an act of consent. Its basic tenor is affirmatory. Essentially it means this: I can affirm the world, being, myself, because I can affirm the ground of my being, for this ground is good. It is good to *be*. Josef Pieper has interpreted the nature of the "feast", the festival (in general terms) as affirmation of the world:[18] whenever I am able to say Yes, I can celebrate a feast; whenever I am able to say Yes, I am (to that extent) free, liberated. Christian prayer holds the key to making the whole world a celebration, a feast, namely, affirmation. Asiatic contemplation is not affirmation but liberation through the renunciation of being. The marxist approach, too, is not affirmation but outrage, opposition to being because it is bad and so must be changed. Prayer is an act of being; it is affirmation, albeit not affirmation of myself as I am and of the world as it is, but affirmation of the ground of being and hence a purifying of myself and of the world from this ground upward. All purification (every *via negationis*) is only possible on the rocklike basis of affirmation, of consent: Jesus Christ is Yes (cf. 2 Cor 1:19f.). Conversely, in the purification which issues from this fundamental Yes we discover the active power of prayer, which (a) yields a deep security in the affirmation of

[18] J. Pieper, *Zustimmung zur Welt. Eine Theorie des Festes* (Munich 1963).

being, as a foil to the hectic world of self-made man, yet which (b) is by no means a flight from the world but rather entrusts people with the task of purifying the world and empowers them to carry it out.

The next step is this: we can only say Abba together with Christ; only in fellowship with him can we recognize the world's ground in a way which invites our Yes. Apart from the Son, the Father remains ambivalent and strange; it is Jesus who turns the scales of the Old Testament and makes its message clear. "Patrocentrism", i.e., the Abba, presupposes the christological character of prayer.[19] It is the Son who guides us along the path of purification which leads to the door of the Yes. So Christian prayer depends on our continually looking to Christ, talking with him, being silent with him, listening to him, doing and suffering with him.

Let us go a step further. We cannot reach Christ through historical reconstruction. It may be helpful, but it is not sufficient and, on its own, becomes mere necrophilia. We encounter him as a living Person only in the foretaste of his presence which is called "Church". At this point we begin to see how it may be possible to purify and accept the inheritance of Asia. The latter is correct in refusing to see individual identity as an encapsulated "I" over against a similarly encapsulated "Thou" of God, ignoring the existence of other "I"s which are themselves related individually and separately to this divine Thou. Here we see the limitation of the kind of personalism which was developed between the Wars by Ebner, Buber, Rosenzweig, E. Brunner, Steinbüchel

[19] Thus we can oppose Harnack's well-known verdict in *Das Wesen des Christentums* that "the Father alone, not the Son, belongs to the gospel which Jesus preached". Harnack is blind to the indirect Christology of Jesus' words, deeds and prayers.

and others. Here God is portrayed in a way which conflicts with his nature as the ground of all being. Partnership between God and man is conceived in I–Thou terms in a way which deprives God of his infinity and excludes each individual "I" from the unity of being. By comparison with God, man's identity is not simply in himself but outside himself, which is why he can only attain it by "transcendence". The Christian believer discovers his true identity in him who, as "the firstborn of all creation", holds all things together (Col 1:15ff.), with the result that we can say that our life is hidden with him in God (Col 3:3).[20] Through identification with Christ I discover my own entirely personal identity.

The Church as a whole presents the model of this kind of "identity". The Church is so identified with Christ that she can be called his "body". But this bodily unity is to be understood against the biblical concept of man and wife: they are to become two in one flesh (Gen 2:24; Eph 5:30f.; cf. 1 Cor 6:16f.). It is a unity through the unifying power of love, which does not destroy the two-ness of I and Thou but welds it into a profound oneness. In finding my own identity by being identified with Christ, I am made one with him; my true self is restored to me, I know that I am accepted, and this enables me to give myself back to him. On this basis the theology of the Middle Ages proposed that the aim of prayer (and the movement of being in which it consists) was that, through it, man should become an *anima ecclesiastica*—a personal embodiment of the Church. This is both identity and purification, it is a surrendering of oneself and a being drawn into the innermost nature of what we mean

[20] Cf. on identity and identification, J. Ratzinger and K. Lehmann, *Mit der Kirche leben* (Freiburg 1977).

by "Church". In this process the language of our Mother becomes ours; we learn to speak it along with her, so that, gradually, her words on our lips become our words. We are given an anticipatory share in the Church's perennial dialogue of love with him who desired to be one flesh with her, and this gift is transformed into the gift of speech. And it is in the gift of speech, and not until then, that I am really restored to my true self; only thus am I given back to God, handed over by him to all my fellow men; only thus am I free.

At this point everything becomes very practical: How can I learn to pray? By praying in fellowship. Prayer is always a praying *with* someone. No one can pray to God as an isolated individual and in his own strength. Isolation and the loss of a basic sense of fellowship in prayer constitute a major reason for the lack of prayer. I learn to pray by praying with others, with my mother for instance, by following her words, which are gradually filled out with meaning for me as I speak, live and suffer in fellowship with her. Naturally I must be always asking what these words mean. Naturally, too, I must continually "cash" these words into the small change of daily life. And having done so, I must try to repossess them in exchange for my small coin, little by little, as I draw nearer the fullness of the mystery and become more capable of speaking of it. And that is precisely why it is impossible to start a conversation with Christ alone, cutting out the Church: a christological form of prayer which excludes the Church also excludes the Spirit and the human being himself. I need to feel my way into these words in everything I do, in prayer, life, suffering, in my thoughts. And this very process transforms me. But I must not try to dispense with the example of the words, for they are alive, a growing organism, words which are lived and prayed by countless people.

Of course, this applies to all the various modes of prayer: repetition, silence, speech, singing and so on. All the dimensions of the human psyche are involved; we must never make the rational understanding the only criterion. How could reason grow and develop if it regarded its own premature limitations as normative![21]

3. Answers to prayer

Christian prayer is addressed to a God who hears and answers. But in what way? What can the witness of the New Testament and the tradition of faith tell us?

a. First let us examine what is meant by answers to prayer.[22] Luke transmits one of the Lord's words which puts it very precisely: "If you then, who are evil, know how to give good gifts to your children, how much more will the heavenly Father give the Holy Spirit to those who ask him?" (Lk 11:13) What we are to ask of God is the gift of the pneuma, his Spirit. God gives himself. We are to ask no less than this. We find the same thing put in different terms in Jesus' farewell discourses in John. Here the gift of God promised unconditionally to those who ask is joy, that "full" joy which is the expression and the presence of a love which has become "full" (Jn 16:24). The reality is the same in each case. Prayer, because of the transformation of being which it involves, means growing more and more into identity with the pneuma of Jesus, the Spirit of God (becoming an *anima ecclesiastica*); borne along by the very breath of his love, we have a joy which cannot be taken from us.

b. But how are we to conceive of God answering

---

[21] Cf. the sections "On the Theological Basis of Church Music" and "On the Structure of the Liturgical Celebration" in this volume.

[22] Cf. J. Ratzinger, *Dogma und Verkündigung* (Munich 1973), 119–32; H. Schaller, op. cit. (note 16 above), 167–90.

prayer? Put in the briefest possible form, we can say something like this: in Jesus, God participates in time. Through this participation he operates in time in the form of love. His love purifies men; through purification (and not otherwise) men are identified and united with him. Or we could say this: as a result of God's participation in time in Jesus, love becomes the causality operating in the world to transform it; in any place, at any time, it can exercise its influence. As a cause, love does not vitiate the world's mechanical causality but uses and adopts it. Love is the power which God exercises in the world. To pray is to put oneself on the side of this love-causality, this causality of freedom, in opposition to the power of necessity. As Christians, as those who pray, this is our very highest task.

Form and Content in
The Eucharistic Celebration

Problematic: The Category of "Form"

If we want to understand the current problems of liturgical reform, we shall need to recall a largely forgotten debate which took place between the two World Wars and which is at the center of these issues. In his book on the Mass, which gave classic expression to the inner experiences and demands of the preceding two decades, Romano Guardini had concentrated on the question of the essential form or structure of the Mass.[1] This development reflected the new liturgical awareness which had been growing in these years. At that time, young people were interested not so much in the inherited dogmatic problems of eucharistic doctrine as in the liturgical celebration as a living form [*Gestalt*]. They found that this form, or structure, was a theological and spiritual entity with an integrity of its own. What previously had been the rubricist's sphere of operations, mere ceremonial, having no apparent connection with dogma, now seemed to be an integral part of the action. It was its actual manifestation, apart from which the reality itself would remain invisible. Some years later Joseph Pascher put it like this: as far as the structure is concerned, up to now people had only paid attention to the rubrics, to what was printed in red; now it was time to give equal attention

---

[1] *Besinnung vor der Feier der heiligen Messe*, 2 vols. (Mainz 1939).

to the red *and* the black print. "There is far more in the form and structure of the texts and the whole celebration than in the rubrics."[2]

Now the structure of the Mass, the form in which it manifests itself, no longer appeared to be a more or less fortuitous collection of ceremonies governed by laws of performance, enveloping a dogmatic core but having no effect upon it. It was seen as the inner expression of the spiritual reality which takes place within the Mass. So it became essential to go behind the contingent individual rites to appreciate the total form which "in-forms" them and which, as such, is the key to what takes place in the Eucharist. Next, this total form or structure could also provide the lever of the reform; it could be used to decide which prayers and gestures were secondary accretions, obscuring rather than revealing the structure. It could be used to determine whether particular aspects were to be heightened or lightened. Thus the concept of form or structure [*Gestalt*], a hitherto unknown category entered the theological dialogue, clearly recognizable as a power for reform. Indeed, it can be said that it was this category that gave birth to liturgical scholarship in the modern sense. For the first time, liturgy appeared as a specific field beside that of dogmatics and canon law, with the result that the issue here was one of theology and a theologically based reform without dogmatics being directly involved. To see the full implications of this development, we need to ask in what terms this fundamental structure was described. There was a very simple way of discovering the structure: the New Testament contains a relatively full account of the

---

[2] J. Pascher, *Eucharistia. Gestalt und Vollzug* (Münster-Krailling 1947), 8.

blueprint of the celebration in the institution of the Eucharist by Jesus himself; it took place on Holy Thursday in the context of the Last Supper. It seemed therefore that the Eucharist's basic structure was un-equivocally that of a meal. No one disputed the fact that Jesus celebrated it as a meal; this, surely, was enough to silence all the critics. "The determining structure is that of the meal", said Joseph Pascher;[3] Guardini and others had already said as much. Protagonists of the liturgical reform were explicitly applying the Lord's "Do this" to the meal structure. People were fond of remarking sar-castically that, after all, Jesus had said, "Do this" and not, "Do what you like."

This kind of talk was bound to stimulate great interest among dogmatic theologians. Was this not the same as Luther's position which was condemned by Trent? Did it not reduce the sacrificial character of the Mass in favor of a meal-oriented theory? Liturgists replied to these accusations by saying that their critics had not appreciated the level of the discussion. To describe the Mass as a sacrifice was a dogmatic statement referring to the hidden theological essence of what takes place in it; to speak of the meal structure, on the other hand, was to direct attention to the visible liturgical per-formance, in no way denying the theological content defined by Trent. What was presented liturgically in the structure of the meal could without difficulty mediate what, dogmatically speaking, was a sacrifice. Ultimately, however, such a simple juxtaposition could not provide a satisfactory answer in the long run. Particularly if the structure is not merely a ceremonial form, but at its core an indispensable manifestation of its essential content, it makes no sense

---

[3] Ibid., 27.

absolutely to separate the one from the other. The lack of clarity which has prevailed in this area, even during the Council, regarding the relation between the dogmatic and liturgical levels, must be regarded as the central problem of the liturgical reform. Failure to deal with it has resulted in a great many of the individual problems which have since preoccupied us.

We must therefore see it as our task to work toward a clarification here—not in purely formal deliberation, but by critically analyzing what is meant by the basic thesis that the Eucharist is fundamentally a meal. This thesis involves a total separation between dogmatic content and liturgical structure, if, indeed, it actually concedes the dogmatic view that the Mass is a sacrifice. But if it should appear that a separation of the two fields cannot be maintained, the thesis itself becomes highly questionable. This became clear at an early stage. In what follows we shall endeavor to trace the stages of the dispute and bring some light to bear on the problem.

We find a first attempt at a reconciliation in Joseph Pascher, who speaks of sacrificial symbolism being introduced into the meal structure. The separation of the gifts of bread and wine, symbolically indicating the fatal spilling of Jesus' blood, introduces the mark of sacrifice into the basic structure of the meal. Of more far-reaching significance, although presented in a restrained vein, was the qualification made by the liturgist J. A. Jungmann. On the basis of the liturgical texts themselves, Jungmann shows that, even in the most ancient forms, the *eucharistia*—the prayer of anamnesis in the shape of a thanksgiving—is more prominent than the meal aspect. According to Jungmann, the basic structure, at least from the end of the first century, is not the meal but the *eucharistia*; even in Ignatius of Antioch this is the term

given to the whole action.[4] In a subsequent study,
Jungmann has gone on to show that, linguistically
speaking, Luther's use of the word "Supper" [*Abendmahl*] was a complete innovation. After 1 Corinthians
11:20 the designation of the Eucharist as a "meal" does
not occur again until the sixteenth century, apart from
direct quotations of 1 Corinthians 11:20 and references
to the satisfaction of hunger (in deliberate contrast to the
Eucharist).[5] Thus the *eucharistia* thesis is able to put the
dogmatic and liturgical levels in touch with each other.
Late antiquity had formulated the concept of the verbal
sacrifice, which even found its way into the Roman
canon under the term *oblatio rationabilis*: sacrifice to the
Divinity does not take place by the transfer of property
but in the self-offering of mind and heart, expressed in
word. This concept was adopted into Christianity without any difficulty. The eucharistic prayer is an entering-in
to the prayer of Jesus Christ himself; hence it is the
Church's entering-in to the Logos, the Father's Word,
into the Logos' self-surrender to the Father, which, in
the Cross, has also become the surrender of mankind to
him.[6] So, on the one hand, *eucharistia* made a bridge to

[4] J. A. Jungmann, *Missarum sollemnia*, 2 vols. (Freiburg 1948–),
I:327ff. [*The Mass of the Roman Rite*, 2 vols. (New York 1951 and
1955)].

[5] Id., " 'Abendmahl' als Name der Eucharistie", in *ZKTh* 93
(1971): 91–94. 93: "Thus it is clear that the term 'Supper' was a
complete innovation in the sixteenth century."

[6] Cf. O. Casel, "Die λογική θυσία der antiken Mystik in christlich-
liturgischer Umdeutung", in *Jahrb. f. Liturgiewissenschaft* 4 (1924):
36ff.; J. Pascher, *Eucharistia* 94–98. Enriching new insights in L.
Bouyer, *Eucharistie. Théologie et spiritualité de la prière eucharistique*
(Tournai 1966) [*Eucharist. Theology and Spirituality of the Eucharistic
Prayer* (London: Notre Dame, 1968)]. Bouyer shows the Jewish
roots of the idea of a verbal sacrifice and thus presents a convincing
picture of the inner unity between Jesus and Church in terms of

Jesus' words of blessing at the Last Supper, in which he actually underwent, in an inward and anticipatory manner, his death on the Cross;[7] and, on the other hand, it built a bridge to the theology of the Logos and hence to a trinitarian deepening of the theology of Eucharist and of the Cross. Ultimately it facilitated the transition to a spiritual concept of sacrifice which was ideally suited to interpret what is special in Jesus' sacrifice. For what we have here is death transformed into a word of acceptance and self-surrender. The il-logical fact of death had become the concern of the Logos: the Logos had died; and as a result, death had become life.

This much should be clear at this stage: if the basic structure of the Mass is not the "meal" but *eucharistia*, there remains a necessary and fruitful difference between the liturgical (structural) and the dogmatic level; but they are not estranged: each seeks and determines the other. Moreover, the meal element is not simply excluded, for *eucharistia* is *also* (but not solely) the grace said before the sacred meal. But the meal symbolism is subordinated to a larger whole and integrated into it. At this point, however, a serious objection arises: it could be said that, once the Church's liturgy has become something tangible, it does not exhibit primarily a meal structure but is subordinated to the "word" dimension of *eucharistia*—as in 1 Corinthians 11, for instance. But does this change the fact that the Last Supper of Jesus was precisely that, a supper? Does this not simply mean that the decline from the pristine form occurred in the very first generation?

---

eucharistia. Cf. also H. U. von Balthasar, "Die Messe, ein Opfer der Kirche?", in id., *Spiritus Creator* (Einsiedeln 1967), 166–217.

[7] Cf. esp. H. Schürmann, *Jesu ureigener Tod. Exegetische Besinnungen und Ausblick* (Freiburg 1975); K. Kertelge (ed.), *Der Tod Jesu im Neuen Testament* (Freiburg 1976); esp. ibid., R. Pesch, "Das Abendmahl und Jesu Todesverständnis", 137–87.

Can there ever be any other standard than that given by Jesus himself, however ancient be contrary Church traditions? As we see, this question leads us into the fundamental problem of current theology, which is marked by the dispute between history and dogma, namely the issue of Jesus versus the Church. To that extent it shares in the fundamental difficulties of Catholic Christianity; it would be surprising if it did not exemplify them in this way. It need hardly be said that the more recent exegesis tends largely to make an increasingly radical separation of the Supper of Jesus and the Church's sacrament and to cut the knot of the Lord's "institution"; this is only a symptom of the same basic problem.[8]

The Growth of the Church and
The Development of the Eucharist

The work of H. Schürmann has been of decisive importance in shedding light on the transition from the Last Supper of Jesus to the Church's Eucharist. Here we cannot enter into the endless controversies which surround the eucharistic tradition: we are deliberately

[8] Characteristic of the present situation is, e.g., R. Feneberg, *Christliche Passafeier und Abendmahl. Eine biblisch-hermeneutische Untersuchung der neutestamentlichen Einsetzungsberichte* (Munich 1971). The current state of research is summarized in the articles "Abendmahl II" (G. Delling) and "Abendmahl III 1" (G. Kretschmar), in *TRE* I:47–89, clearly indicating a return to continuity between Jesus and the Church's Eucharist; cf. also G. Kretschmar, "Abendmahlsfeier I", in *TRE* I:229–78. Notable exegetical works in the same direction are H. Patsch, *Abendmahl und historischer Jesus* (Stuttgart 1972) and R. Pesch, *Wie Jesus das Abendmahl hielt. Der Grund der Eucharistie* (Freiburg 1977). For a systematic presentation of the subject in an ecumenical perspective, cf. the magnificent article "Abendmahl IV" by U. Kühn, in *TRE* I:145–212.

restricting our enquiry to the structure [*Gestalt*] and its development, and in this regard Schürmann has identified three stages: 1. the Eucharist at the Last Supper of Jesus; 2. the Eucharist in connection with the apostolic community meal; 3. the celebration of the Eucharist in postapostolic times, separated from the community meal.[9] Unfortunately there is not space here to reproduce the details of the process; we can only mention the critical transitions and examine their inner significance. As far as the Eucharist at the Last Supper of Jesus is concerned, it is possible to reconstruct the locus of Jesus' eucharistic actions fairly precisely through recourse to the Gospels and Jewish meal customs. Assuming that the meal in question was a Passover supper, it had a fourfold structure encompassing a small preliminary meal, the Passover liturgy, the main meal, and the concluding rites. The breaking of bread took place therefore before the main meal itself; the giving of the cup follows the main meal, as Luke expressly says: "*after* supper" (22:20). Schürmann concludes two things from this: "1. At the Last Supper the eucharistic action was an *integral and constitutive part of a meal-structure*. . . . 2. At the Last Supper the eucharistic action had a *relatively autonomous existence and significance* in contrast to the meal event."[10] What the Lord is doing here is something new. It is woven into an old context—that of the Jewish ritual meal—but it is clearly recognizable as an independent entity. He commanded it to be repeated, which implies that it was separable from the immediate context in which it took place.

[9] H. Schürmann, "Die Gestalt der urchristlichen Eucharistiefeier", in id., *Ursprung und Gestalt. Erörterungen und Besinnungen zum Neuen Testament* (Düsseldorf 1970), 77–99.

[10] Ibid., 83f.

There is nothing fortuitous in this interplay of old and new. It is the exact and necessary expression of the existing situation in salvation history. Jesus prays his new prayer within the Jewish liturgy. The crucifixion has not yet taken place, even though, in a way, it has begun. Jesus has not yet become separated from the Jewish community, i.e., the Church as Church has not yet come into being; "Church" in the narrower historical sense does not come about until the attempt to win the whole of Israel has failed. Since, as yet, there is no independent Christian reality, but only an open-ended form within Judaism, there cannot be an independent and specifically Christian form of liturgy. The real mistake of those who attempt uncritically to deduce the Christian liturgy directly from the Last Supper lies in their failing to see this fundamental point: the Last Supper of Jesus is certainly the basis of all Christian liturgy, but in itself it is not yet Christian. The act constituting the Christian reality takes place *within* the Jewish framework, but it has not yet attained a form, a structure [*Gestalt*] of its own as Christian liturgy. Salvation history is still open-ended; no definitive decision has been made as to whether the Christian phenomenon will or will not have to separate itself from its Jewish matrix as a distinct reality. Indeed, we could make the issue clearer by taking the earlier suggestions of the liturgical movement and turning them upside down: the Last Supper is the foundation of the dogmatic content of the Christian Eucharist, not of its liturgical form. The latter does not yet exist. As her separation from Israel became unavoidable, the Church had to discover an appropriate form of her own in which to express the reality bequeathed to her. This is a necessity arising out of the situation, not a decline. This seems to me to be a crucial point, not only for the debate about the liturgical form, but for a genuine understanding of the Christian reality. The idea that, after Jesus, there was an immediate decline in primitive Christianity, resulting in the hiatus between Jesus and the Church which still persists today,[11] rests on a failure to take these facts into account. If this is the case, there *can* be no direct continuity between Jesus and the Church; this is also why the proclamation of the word has moved its center of gravity from the "Kingdom of God" to Christology.[12] In this situation, unity with Jesus has to be sought in that discontinuity which is manifested where the proclamation of the Kingdom to Israel is left behind and the Church of the Gentiles is embraced.

Now let us turn to the second phase of the development traced by Schürmann, the apostolic Eucharist connected with the community meal. For the sake of brevity I go straight to the core of Schürmann's description of this phase: "The primitive Christian community meal was not a repetition of the Last Supper of Jesus (which is not what Jesus commanded to be repeated); it was the continuation of Jesus' everyday table fellowship with his disciples. . . . Faced with the issue of incorporating Jesus' twofold eucharistic action into this community meal, the more obvious course was to insert the two actions together rather than to place them before and after their usual meal."[13] Two things here are important for our present consideration: first of all it is clear that Jesus' command to repeat the action does not refer to the Last Supper as a

[11] The picture of Jesus given in H. Küng's *On Being a Christian* (Doubleday 1976) is in many respects symptomatic of this. Cf. my observations in the collection *Diskussion über Hans Küngs "Christ sein"* (Mainz 1976), 7–18.

[12] Further details in J. Ratzinger, *Eschatologie* (Regensburg 1977), 30–42.

[13] Ibid., 85.

whole at all, but to the specifically eucharistic action. Thus the Last Supper was not repeated, and this in itself caused a change in the overall structure and gave birth to a specifically Christian form. An ordinary meal precedes the eucharistic celebration; the eucharistic acts, now joined together, follow in the form of a distinct action, framed and heightened by the prayer of thanksgiving, *eucharistia*. This sequence is clearly visible in 1 Corinthians 11:17–34, but it is also perceptible in the way Matthew and Mark "match" the words spoken at the giving of the bread and of the cup. At one point, however, we must disagree with Schürmann. His thesis, that the apostolic Eucharist is a continuation of Jesus' daily table fellowship with his disciples, was limited to the question of the structural origin of the celebration, but it is used by many people who wish to deny that anything was "instituted" at the Last Supper and who assume that the Eucharist originated more or less exclusively in Jesus' meals with sinners. This view identifies the Eucharist of Jesus with a strictly Lutheran doctrine of justification, namely, the pardoning of the sinner; ultimately, among those who see Jesus' eating with sinners as the only solid fact about the historical Jesus which has come down to us, the whole of Christology and theology is reduced to this one factor.[14] It results in a view of the Eucharist

[14] This is the tendency of several studies by E. Fuchs, e.g., *Das urchristliche Sakramentsverständnis* (Schriftenreihe der Kirchlich-Theologischen Sozietät in Württemberg, Heft 8, 1958); cf. the remarks of J. M. Robinson on this issue in his *New Quest of the Historical Jesus* (London 1969). The conception of the Eucharist in W. Pannenberg tends somewhat in the same direction; cf. his (otherwise most helpful) study "Die Problematik der Abendmahlslehre aus evangelischer Sicht", in G. Krems/R. Mumm (ed.), *Evangelisch-katholische Abendmahlsgemeinschaft?* (Regensburg/Göttingen 1971), 9–45; W. Pannenberg, *Thesen zur Theologie der Kirche* (Munich 1970), esp. theses 77 and 85, pp. 34 and 36.

which has nothing in common with primitive Christianity. Whereas Paul says that those who approach the Eucharist in sin "eat and drink judgment" upon themselves (1 Cor 11:29) and pronounces an anathema to protect the Eucharist from abuse (1 Cor 16:22), proponents of this view see it as the essence of the Eucharist that it is available to all without distinction and without conditions. It is interpreted as the sign of the unconditional grace of God, offered directly to sinners and even to unbelievers—but at this point it certainly has little in common with Luther's understanding of the Eucharist. The fact that this thesis contradicts the entire eucharistic inheritance of the New Testament indicates the wrongheadedness of its basic assumption: the Christian Eucharist was not understood in the context of Jesus' eating with sinners, nor can it be seen simply as a continuation of his daily table fellowship with the disciples. There are two reasons for this:

a. First, as Schürmann himself observes, there is the festal quality of the Eucharist. Through the provision of wine, it was lifted from everyday ordinariness and shown to be a festal celebration. There is no evidence that the Eucharist was celebrated daily in apostolic times, as Schürmann's thesis would suggest. We must assume a weekly celebration; indeed, as Revelation 1:10 (cf. Acts 20:7; 1 Cor 16:2) indicates, a Sunday Eucharist.[15]

b. The second reason against this interpretation is the firm outline of the Eucharist, based on the Passover ritual. Just as the Passover meal was celebrated in a clearly defined household, the Eucharist too, from the

---

[15] This does not impugn the Western custom of daily Eucharist, which can certainly be traced back to the third century. This development could easily take place once the Christian liturgy had discovered its own special form.

beginning, had definite conditions for admission. From the start, Eucharist was celebrated in what one might call the household of Jesus Christ, and thus it built the "Church".

The situation, then, is highly nuanced. As such, the Christian Eucharist is not a repetition of the Last Supper (which was in fact unique). If the latter was a Passover meal, for which there is much evidence, it cannot have been repeated, for Passover occurs once a year according to the lunar calendar, whereas the Eucharist is celebrated weekly. On the other hand the Eucharist does take over substantial elements from the Passover tradition, not least the festal atmosphere and the precise admission conditions. Right from the apostolic period it clearly begins to construct its own special form. We might put it like this: the eucharistic actions are taken out of the context of the Passover and are placed within the new context of the "Lord's Day", i.e., the day which marked the first meeting with the Risen Lord. The appearance of the Risen Lord to those who are his is the new beginning, causing the Jewish calendar of feasts to be left behind as obsolete and situating the gift of the Eucharist in its new setting. To that extent Sunday, the first day of the week (also regarded as the first day of creation and now marking the new creation) is the real inner locus of the Eucharist as a Christian form [*Gestalt*]. Sunday and Eucharist belong together right from the beginning; the day of the Resurrection is the matrix of the Eucharist.[16]

[16] Very important observations on the connection between Eucharist and Sunday are to be found in J. J. von Allmen, *Ökumene im Herrenmahl* (Kassel 1968), 20f.

This is the situation, therefore, in the second phase: the new, Christian elements are taken out of the context of the Last Supper, joined together and placed after the disciples' fellowship meal. Meal and Eucharist are linked by the fundamental Christian idea of agape. The mutual agape of the community provides the context for the transforming agape of the Lord. However, the actual development of the communities cannot match this ideal vision. What in fact happened was that the community agape, which had been meant to open the door to the Lord, became an occasion for egoism. Thus it proved unsuitable as a preparation for the meeting with Christ. This resulted in the separation of meal and Eucharist, as documented in 1 Corinthians 11:22: "Have you not houses to eat and drink in?" This development will have taken place at a different speed in different places, but it signifies the start of the third phase, resulting in the final ecclesial form of the sacrament.[17] We find the first witness to this form in the letter of Pliny to Trajan which speaks of the morning celebration of the Eucharist.[18] Justin Martyr (d. ca. 165) gives us the first full description of the new form. Sunday morning proves to be the Christians' time for worship, underlining the connection between the service of worship and the event of the Resurrection. Separation from the Jewish matrix and the independent existence of the Christian reality, which began with the Christians' commitment to assemble on the Lord's day, have become definitive by the fixing of the time for worship. But there is a further consequence: as long as

[17] Cf. Schürmann, "Die Gestalt der urchristlichen Eucharistiefeier", 92, esp. note 77; on the theological problems connected with the agape, cf. J. J. von Allmen, op. cit., 69–75.

[18] Cf. Schürmann, 92.

the Eucharist immediately followed a community meal, participation in the synagogue's service of the word was presupposed. Very early on (though not from the beginning), Christians had withdrawn from the Temple sacrifice; but they did assemble in Solomon's Portico, continuing to share, there and in the synagogues, in the service of readings and prayer of the people of Israel. Within this service they had tried to explain their interpretation of Scripture, i.e., the Old Testament, by reference to Christ, hoping to make the entire Bible, without loss, the Lord's.[19] John's Gospel belongs to a period when a complete and final break had occurred.[20] Now a distinct, Christian service of the word had to be created, and this was joined to the eucharistic celebration, resulting in the growth of a coherent Christian liturgy. The inner rationale of the resultant liturgical pattern is presented in the account of the disciples on the road to Emmaus (Lk 24:25–31). First we have the searching of the Scriptures, explained and made present by the Risen Lord; their minds enlightened, the disciples are moved to invite the Lord to stay with them, and he responds by breaking the bread for his disciples, giving them his presence and then withdrawing again, sending them out as his messengers. This coherent and integrated form arose quite naturally when the Church was no longer able to participate in synagogue worship and thus acquired an identity and a form of her own, as the community of believers in Christ.

One can hardly allot a single term to a reality which

[19] Cf. F. Mussner, "Die Una Sancta nach Apg 2, 42", in id., *Praesentia salutis* (Düsseldorf 1967), 212–22; J. Ratzinger, "Auferbaut aus lebendigen Steinen", in W. Seidel, *Kirche aus lebendigen Steinen* (Mainz 1975), 30–48, esp. 39f. and 43, note 12.

[20] Cf. on this issue, R. Leistner, *Antijudaismus im Johannesevangelium?* (Frankfurt 1974).

has grown in this way to become the norm for all liturgical development in Christendom—and the whole thrust of this liturgy means that it must remain normative. Schürmann too comes to this conclusion, although, as far as the question of form and structure is concerned, he feels obliged to separate the liturgy of the word from eucharistic liturgy in the narrower sense. Initially he speaks of a meal structure in course of development. But even when he has kept the liturgy of the word out of the discussion—a questionable decision—his concept of meal structure is subject to so many qualifications that it disintegrates. First of all he says, "We are somewhat uneasy about applying the term 'meal structure' to the eucharistic action described by Justin",[21] and he defines the outer limits of the term: in the first place the meal structure is so strongly stylized that one can only speak of a "symbolic" meal. This fact is evident in the posture of those celebrating the Eucharist: whereas they sit for the service of the word, they *stand* for the eucharistic action, which certainly does not indicate the transition to a normal meal situation. Furthermore the prayer, the *eucharistia*, has become so dominant that Schürmann feels obliged to describe the "symbolic" meal structure as "impaired".[22] It would show greater objectivity, under these conditions, simply to abandon the inappro-

[21] Schürmann, op. cit., 95.

[22] Op. cit., 92–95. Schürmann makes a useful comparison (96): "A great number of the parables of Jesus share a distinctive feature: at a certain point the image does not fit; it is exaggerated, becomes paradoxical, grotesque, improbable. And this is the very point of contact between the image and what lies behind it; it is where the reality shines through the image and bursts it. Similarly, the over-emphasis on the eucharistic prayer at the eucharistic meal causes what lies behind the meal to shine through." Once again, apropos, it is clear that the concept of the "meal structure" is inappropriate.

priate term "meal structure". The determining element
is the *eucharistia*. Since this is a participation in the
thanksgiving of Jesus, which includes the prayer of
gratitude for the gifts of the earth, it already expresses
whatever element of the "meal" the liturgical action
actually contains.

The analysis of the historical development thus confirms and deepens the thesis cautiously put forward by
Jungmann on the basis of the liturgical sources. At the
same time it has become clear that, while we must reject
the idea that the Christian liturgy originates simply in
the Last Supper, there is no hiatus between Jesus and the
Church. The Lord's gift is not some rigid formula but a
living reality. It was open to historical development, and
only where this development is accepted can there be
continuity with Jesus. Here, as so often, "progressive"
reformers exhibit a fundamentally narrow view of
Christian beginnings, seeing history piecemeal, whereas
the sacramental view of the Church rests upon an inner
developmental unity. It is precisely by pressing forward
that this unity keeps faith and brings into one, by the
power and gift of the one Lord, all the changing times of
history. This formal aspect, as well as the actual content,
can be of great importance for the Church in her contemporary struggles. Once the concept of the "meal"
is seen to be historically a crass oversimplification, once
the Lord's testament is correctly seen in terms of *eucharistia*,
many of the current theories just fade away. And above
all it puts an end to the baneful isolation of the liturgical
and dogmatic levels, without confusing what is specific
to each level. Thus *eucharistia* is the gift of *communio* in
which the Lord becomes our food; it also signifies the
self-offering of Jesus Christ, perfecting his trinitarian
Yes to the Father by his consent to the Cross, and

reconciling us all to the Father in this "sacrifice". There is no opposition between "meal" and "sacrifice"; they belong inseparably together in the new sacrifice of the Lord.

Postscript 1

The issues raised in the foregoing brief study have since been taken up and extended by L. Lies in "Eulogia— Überlegungen zur formalen Sinngestalt der Eucharistie", in *ZKTh* 100 (1978): 69–97, including an appendix of relevant reviews (98–126). What I have called form, structure [*Gestalt, Grundgestalt*] in common with liturgical scholars of the interwar and postwar period, Lies refers to as the "material structure" [*Materialgestalt*], going on to inquire as to the formal structure [*Formalgestalt*], which he defines thus: "By the formal structure of the Eucharist we mean that structure which is able to embrace the ideas of anamnesis, sacramental Real Presence, sacrifice and meal, imparting to all aspects of the Eucharist their formal meaning" (69). Lies discovers this formal structure in the concept of *eulogia*. "As the auto-eulogia of God, Jesus enters into the form of the Old Testament Passover-eulogia; he presents himself as this Passover-eulogia. This is the essential vehicle of meaning [*Sinngestalt*] of the Church's Eucharist. Thus the idea of *eulogia* is able to embrace that christological concentration which systematic theologians require in the doctrine of the Eucharist. Since the Lord's Supper is something that takes place here and now, under the sign of blessing, it embraces both the Real Presence aspect and the aspect of eulogic anamnesis. The Eucharist exhibits a sacrificial structure in a twofold sense. . . . The concept of *eulogia* can provide an integrated model for the Christian

Eucharist, expressing both its theological and its liturgical meaning" (96). I am in full agreement with Lies'
remarks: I find they confirm and enrich my own conclusions. My own enquiry was concerned, however, with
an earlier stage of the argument. Whereas he presupposes
the developed structure of anamnesis, sacramental Real
Presence, sacrifice and meal, my own concern was to
establish the legitimacy of the transition from the Last
Supper to the Mass, from Jesus to the Church's Eucharist.
For this is the salient point of the whole discussion in
contemporary theology. It determines the view of Jesus
and the Church, the relation of pre-Easter to post-Easter
kerygma and the concept of tradition and Church
development.

Because of our distinct approaches, therefore, our
fundamental agreement as to results seems all the more
significant. People should no longer be able to speak of
the Eucharist's "meal structure" *tout court*, since such a
view is based on a misunderstanding of the Eucharist's
origins and leads to a false view of the sacrament. There
is even less excuse for the Eucharist being referred to
simply as a "meal" (or even as a "sacrificial meal"). In
this regard there is an urgent need to revise the German
translation of the Missal of Paul VI, where, in the post-
communion prayers, contrary to the Latin original, the
word "meal" [*Mahl*] is almost used as a regular term
for the Eucharist.

Postscript 2

A whole new perspective has been opened up by the
seminal study by H. Gese entitled "Die Herkunft des
Herrenmahls" [The Origin of the Lord's Supper] in

his book *Zur biblischen Theologie* (Munich 1977), 107–27. This most stimulating article not only confirms the basic thesis presented here but extends its scope in a totally unforeseen manner. Gese begins by taking issue with the still current hypothesis that there were two forms of the Lord's Supper: a sacramental, Hellenistic form and a non-sacramental, Jewish form associated with Jerusalem— a hypothesis in no way supported by the texts themselves. "Behind this hypothesis is a further problem: for it is held that the sacramental view cannot have evolved from the Jewish view" (109). It is this contradiction which causes Gese to take up the question of origins again, as a result of which he comes down in favor of the eucharistic view.

First he discusses the various origins proposed, such as the Jewish meal, the Passover, the Qumran meals, Jesus' meals, the miraculous feedings, the meals of the Risen Jesus. He is able to show that none of these proposed solutions does justice to the evidence of the New Testament. Thus, for instance, the miracles of feeding and the (anti-Docetic) meals of the Risen Lord, "far from explaining the Lord's Supper, in fact presuppose it" (117). In the Passion narratives the death of Jesus is already presented as a Passover sacrifice, as a "saving Passover-event of liberation and new birth out of the chaos of the old world" (114); but this by no means implies that the Lord's Supper is identified with the Passover or can be traced back to it. The results show that, while the Passover came to be very important for an understanding of Christ's Passion and hence acquired a fundamental significance in the theology of the Eucharist, it is impossible, all the same, to deduce the Eucharist from it.

The Passover meal is a specific form of the Jewish

ritual meal. Before going on to examine the various
alternative forms, therefore, we must establish the theological content of the Jewish ritual meal in general and
see what kind of bridges exist between it and the Eucharist.
At this point Gese brings to light a number of striking
facts. "The Jewish meal exhibits several basic character-
istics, arising from the fact that the celebratory meal was
associated in ancient times with a primary form of sacrifice,
the *zēbaḥ*. In pre-Deuteronomic times, the slaughter of
animals could only take place at the altar. Therefore the
eating of meat presupposed a sacrificial context. . . .
Bread and wine were, however, basic constituents, and
these unbloody elements did not of themselves presuppose
an altar. The sacrificial character of this meal has a
twofold significance: it expresses communion with God,
in whose sacrifice people are permitted to share, and
communion among the participants; these two things
correspond to the saving fact that *shalom* reigns among
those who share in the sacrificial meal (which is why
these sacrifices, celebrated as a public, liturgical feast, are
called *šelamim*, "peace offerings") (109f.). One is reminded
of the ancient Church's designation of the Eucharist as
pax, continuing the tradition of Israel, which itself reflects
a fundamental human tradition. There is another important fact: the ancient ritual meal—which always begins
with the *berakah*, the blessing pronounced over bread
and wine—"inaugurates . . . a being-in-peace". Thus
the raising of the cup acquires a special meaning, for it is
associated with the ritual proclamation initiating this
particular mode of being. "Thus the sacrificial meal is
given its particular meaning from the particular circumstances in which it is celebrated. In Exodus 24:11 it
inaugurates the covenant between Yahweh and Israel on
Sinai; in Isaiah 25:1–10 the new covenant on Sion is

established by the meal—here in the special form of the thanksgiving sacrifice. A great variety of ritual meals can be envisaged" (110).

Here we are faced once more with the question: what was the special meal which was able to develop into the Lord's Eucharist? Gese observes: "Strangely enough, one particular form of the ritual meal which is deeply rooted in the Old Testament and which also played a prominent part in Judaism at the time of Jesus (according to the Mishnah) has been neglected by scholars: the *tōda*, 'thanksgiving sacrifice'. This sacrifice is in the category of *zēbaḥ*, it is a sacrificial meal in the wider sense, but it differs considerably from the general sacrificial meal as far as the ritual and the theological significance are concerned. We have been looking for a link with the death and saving activity of the offerer. Here it is" (117). As to the influence of this kind of sacrificial meal, we can say "that the *tōda* formed the cultic basis of the major part of the Psalter" (119). As examples of *tōda* psalms (psalms which have their *sitz im leben* in a celebration of *tōda*), Gese analyzes Psalms 69; 51; 40:1–12 and 22—the great christological psalms of the New Testament. (Indeed, for the evangelists, Psalm 22 became a textbook on the Passion of Christ.) From the context revealed by Gese, it is clear that what we have here is not some retrospective application of Old Testament words to an event, transforming and "theologizing" it: the Passion and Resurrection of Jesus *is tōda*. It is the real fulfillment of the words of these psalms at a new depth. Indeed, it is as if the words had been waiting for their profound fulfillment in Jesus, a fulfillment which surpasses every individual destiny, whether of death or of deliverance, and which also surpasses the merely collective destiny of

Israel, expanding both individual and collective destinies into something far greater and hitherto unknown.

What is *tōda*? Gese describes it like this: "The thanksgiving sacrifice presupposes a particular *situation*. If a man is saved from death, from fatal illness or from those who seek his life, he celebrates this divine deliverance in a service of thanksgiving which marks an existential new start in his life. In it, he "confesses" (*jd*[*h*]) God to be his deliverer by celebrating a thankoffering (*tōda*). He invites his friends and associates, provides the sacrificial animal . . . and celebrates . . . together with his invited guests, the inauguration of his new existence. . . . In order to recall God's deliverance and give thanks for it, it is necessary to reflect on one's pilgrimage through suffering, to bring to mind the process of redemption. . . . It is not a mere sacrificial rite; it is a sacrifice in which one professes one's involvement. . . . Here we have a unity which embraces a service of the word and a ritual meal, praise and sacrifice. The sacrifice cannot be misunderstood as a 'gift' to God; rather it is a way of 'honoring' the Deliverer. And the fact that the rescued man is able to celebrate 'life restored' in the sacred meal is itself the gift of God" (117f.).

As regards the formal elements, two factors are particularly important in the present context. As we have already noted, this type of sacrifice is a "confession of thanksgiving". "Once the confession of divine deliverance had become a constitutive part of the sacrifice, this rite could be seen as complementing the sacrifice itself. The cup corresponds to the proclamatory aspect of the *tōda*, the sacrifice corresponds to its meal aspect" (118). Here we come across the Hellenistic idea of verbal sacrifice, to which we have already referred where we spoke of the Eucharist as the structural element and vehicle of the sacrifice concept. It is an idea we find deeply rooted in the Old Testament, bursting forth from the inner dynamism of Old Testament faith. It is a bridge, already in existence, linking the Old Testament and Jesus to the "nations", to the Greek world. Here distinct developments of the human mind are in touch with one another; it is as if both the Jewish and the Hellenistic traditions are awaiting him who is himself the Word, the crucified Logos, and the Righteous One who has been rescued from the abyss of death. The second important formal element concerns what nowadays we call the "matter" of the sacrament: "The *tōda* is not restricted to a bloody sacrifice of flesh but also embraces the unbloody offering of bread; *tōda* is the only form of sacrifice which is concerned with unleavened bread. Thus in the context of *tōda*, bread and wine acquire a special significance; the one becomes part of the sacrifice itself, the other plays a constitutive role in proclamation" (119).

I would like to draw attention to just two points from Gese's analysis of the *tōda* psalms. First, from Psalm 51: "The sacrifice acceptable to God is a broken spirit; a broken and contrite heart, O God, thou wilt not despise" (v. 17). Here we find "the external sacrifice of the *tōda* interiorized: it has become the sacrificial suffering of one's own life" (120). We can see how "the understanding of sacrifice and the understanding of life have influenced one another through the *tōda* spirituality". In Psalm 40:1–12 the same idea is present in an intensified form: "In connection with the idea of the New Covenant (Jer 31:33; Ez 36:27), the goal is now the total interiorizing of the torah. What we find in the Psalms is not a kind of rationalistic criticism of sacrifice; it is a view of man's total involvement in the very nature of the sacrifice, arising from a deeply rooted spirituality of the thankoffering" (121).

The second point is connected especially with Psalms 22 and 69. Here the mortal suffering of the praying worshipper seems to be "heightened to an ultimate of suffering"; correspondingly, "the experienced deliverance also bursts all historical bounds. . . . It became the sign of the eschatological inauguration of the *basileia*. In the apocalyptic perspective, the fundamental experience of *tōda* spirituality, namely, death and redemption, was lifted to the level of an absolute. Deliverance from death led to the world being converted, the dead partaking of life and salvation being preached to all nations (Ps 22:28ff.)" (121).

Anyone who takes account of these factors will not find it difficult to understand the origins of the Eucharist of Jesus Christ. Structurally speaking, the whole of Christology, indeed the whole of eucharistic Christology, is present in the *tōda* spirituality of the Old Testament. As Gese sums it up: "The Lord's Supper is the *tōda* of the Risen One" (122). We need not go into every detail of this transposition here. But it is important to point out the crucial deepening of the Old Testament *tōda* sacrifice, a development which is entirely consonant with its inner intentionality and which thus transforms the Old Covenant into the New: "In the old *tōda* the man who had experienced deliverance provided a sacrificial animal as a sacrifice for himself and the community. However, the Risen Lord has given himself; the sacrifice is *his* sacrifice, his physical, earthly existence, offered up for us. . . . Because of its sacredness as a sacrifice, the food of the sacred meal represented by the sacrificial bread is the body of Jesus. . . . The bread does not signify the body of Jesus in a metaphorical sense; in its very nature, as the substance of the meal eaten in *tōda* sacrifice, it is the sacrifice of Jesus" (123).

The *tōda* of Jesus vindicates the rabbinic dictum: "In the coming (Messianic) time, all sacrifices will cease except the *tōda* sacrifice. This will never cease in all eternity. All (religious) song will cease too, but the songs of *tōda* will never cease in all eternity" (quoted by Gese, 122).

I have reproduced the context of Gese's study in some detail because I feel that its importance cannot be overestimated. It puts the dispute over the question of sacrifice, which has separated Christendom for more than four centuries, in an entirely different light. Surely there are new possibilities here for the ecumenical dialogue between Catholics and Protestants? For it gives us a genuinely New Testament concept of sacrifice that both preserves the complete Catholic inheritance (and imparts to it a new profundity) and, on the other hand, is receptive to Luther's central intentions. Such a synthesis is possible because the inner unity of both Testaments has been brought to light, a unity of which modern theology had increasingly lost sight, whereas the New Testament itself wished to be no more than the complete and full understanding of the Old Testament, now made possible in Christ. The whole Old Testament is a movement of transition to Christ, a waiting for the One in whom all its words would come true, in whom the "Covenant" would attain fulfillment as the New Covenant. Here too, finally, we can see the meaning of the Real Presence and the entire theology of the Easter worship of Christianity against the biblical background of salvation history. Just as this analysis has shown us the unity of the Old and New Testament, of the Catholic and the Protestant inheritance, so too it reveals the unity of the Bible and the faith of the Church, of theology and pastoral practice. Thus I would also like to quote the warning which Gese addresses to those engaged in pastoral practice: ". . . Let no one imagine that we can help modern man by cutting down on the sacramental dimension. The reverse is the case. People have been cutting down for a long time now, and this is what has caused so many misunderstandings. The only way really to help is to expound this central service of worship fully and in a positive spirit. And as for experimentation, it is *least* appropriate where the liturgy of the Lord's Supper is concerned . . ." (127).

The conclusion that *eucharistia*, or *eulogia*, is the determining "form" of the Eucharist has been confirmed in a startling way by Gese's study. For the first time we can see clearly the full content of the Eucharist and what follows from it. For the moment we can leave aside the question of the various corrections and additions which may prove necessary as a result of scholarly response to Gese's work.[1] It seems to me that his central insight, that is, the close connection between *tōda* sacrifice and

[1] Shortly before his death J. Jeremias took up a decidedly negative position in his short article "Ist das Dankopfermahl der Ursprung des Herrenmahls?", in C. K. Barrett/L. Bammel/W. D. Davies (ed.), *Donum Gentilicium. New Testament Studies in Honour of David Daube* (London 1977), 64–67. Unfortunately Jeremias was dealing, not with the study by Gese which we have presented here, but with Gese's earlier study "Psalm 22 und das Neue Testament. Der älteste Bericht vom Tode Jesu und die Entstehung des Herrenmahls", in *ZThK* 65 (1968): 1–22. This earlier study manifested neither the full content of Gese's theses nor his full reasons substantiating them. In a letter to me, Professor Gese has kindly indicated, in considerable detail, his response to the objections of Jeremias and has disposed of them convincingly. In particular Gese clearly refutes Jeremias' suggestion that the location of the *tōda* psalms in the institution of *tōda* sacrifice is Gese's own (unproven) theory. On the contrary, it is a "view common in Old Testament scholarship ever since Gunkel's study of literary types". And whereas Jeremias had adduced a Mishnah rule to the effect that "thankofferings were most strictly forbidden during the week of

Eucharist, *tōda* spirituality and Christology, is completely sound. The close connection made, in the New Testament tradition, between the *tōda* psalms and Christology, the structural unity between these psalms and the content of the Eucharist—these things are so obvious that, on the basis of the New Testament texts, they cannot be disputed.

Easter", Gese replies with a contrary text, showing that the rule admitted of exceptions.

If I were to question Gese, I should do so on the following lines: the *tōda* sacrifice is the thanksgiving of the man who has already been delivered; in a real sense, surely, it cannot take place until after the Resurrection. This would fit perfectly with the thesis I have presented, namely, that Eucharist is only possible at the Last Supper in an anticipatory form, and that therefore it cannot be a simple development of the Last Supper alone. The Last Supper looks to the Cross, where Jesus' words of self-offering will be fulfilled, and to the hope of Resurrection. Apart from them it would be incomplete and, indeed, unreal. Again, this means that the form of the Last Supper is not complete in itself. If we trace the Eucharist back to the institution of *tōda*, it becomes impossible to see it as a development of the Last Supper alone. In view of *tōda*, the form of the Last Supper must be an "open" form, since *tōda* does not become a reality until it is complemented by Cross and Resurrection.

On the Structure of the Liturgical Celebration

The crisis in the liturgy (and hence in the Church) in which we find ourselves has very little to do with the change from the old to the new liturgical books. More and more clearly we can see that, behind all the conflicting views, there is a profound disagreement about the very nature of the liturgical celebration, its antecedents, its proper form, and about those who are responsible for it. The issue concerns the basic structure of all liturgy, and, whether we are aware of it or not, two fundamentally different views are involved. The basic concepts of the new view are creativity, freedom, celebration and community. It sees things like rite, obligation, interiority and church order as negative factors, belonging to the "old" liturgy which is to be superseded. Here is an illustration, chosen at random, of this "new" view of liturgy: "Liturgy is not some officially prescribed ritual but a concrete celebration, fashioned as an authentic expression of the celebrating community, with the minimum of external control. Liturgy is not a specifically ecclesiastical cult with its own spirituality, to be performed in an objective manner. . . . The priest's missal is his guidebook for his particular role . . . and in a similar way, *Gotteslob* [the congregational music book] is the congregation's guidebook. Liturgy is created in a particular place at a particular time; this emphasizes the role of the community. . . . Since the Council, a higher value has been placed on the congregation's singing. No longer does the reality exist *behind* the singing: what is sung *is* the reality. . . ."[1]

The fundamental idea here is that liturgy is a community celebration, an act in which the community forms and experiences itself as such. In fact this means that the liturgy more and more acquires a "party" character and atmosphere, as we see for instance in the increased importance attached to the words of greeting and dismissal and in the search for elements with "entertainment" value. A "successful" liturgical celebration is judged by the effects achieved in this way. Liturgy is thus dependent on the "creativity", the "ideas" of those who organize it.

I. The Nature of the Liturgical Celebration

The fact that this approach, consistently carried out, would destroy liturgy, that is, the common public worship of the Church, must not obscure the fact that it is right about *one* fundamental element, namely, the "celebratory" character of liturgy. Here is common ground for a discussion of the structure of liturgy. Strictly speaking we should say that liturgy, of its nature, has a festal character.[2] If we can agree on this starting point, the issue then becomes: What makes a feast a feast? Evidently, for the view in question, the festal quality is

[1] E. Bickl, "Zur Rezeption des 'Gotteslob'. Einführungsschwierigkeiten und Lesungsvorschläge", in *Singende Kirche* 25 (1977/78): 115–18.

[2] Cf. J. Ratzinger, *Eucharistie—Mitte der Kirche* (Munich 1978), 37f. On the subject of the feast, cf. again J. Pieper, *Zustimmung zur Welt. Eine Theorie des Festes*, 2nd ed. (Munich 1964).

guaranteed by the concrete "community" experience of a group of people who have grown together into this community. What facilitates this experience of community, what it expresses, in this view, is spontaneity and free expression, i.e., the departure from the fixed routine of everyday life, the creativity expressing what animates the community as community. Here liturgy means "playing" with the various roles, with everyone "playing" together and creating the "celebration". Again it seems to me that there *is* an element of truth in this, namely, the idea that central to the "feast" is the freedom whereby we extract ourselves from the constraints of everyday life, and that in this way the feast creates a foundation for community. However, if we are really to be made free, we need also to break out of the restrictions of "roles"; we need to lay them aside and allow our real selves to come to light. Otherwise it all remains a game, a more or less beautiful veneer, holding us at a superficial level and, far from facilitating freedom and community, obstructing them.

This being so, all civilizations have found that those who celebrate a feast need some external motive empowering them to do so. They cannot do it of themselves. There needs to be a reason for the feast, an objective reason prior to the individual's will. In other words, I can only celebrate freedom if I *am* free; otherwise it is tragic self-delusion. I can only celebrate joy if the world and human existence really give me reason to rejoice. *Am* I free? *Is* there cause for joy? Where these questions are excluded, the "party"—the post-religious world's attempt to rediscover the feast—is soon revealed as a tragic masquerade. It is no coincidence that, wherever people go to parties looking for "redemption", i.e., the experience of liberation from self-alienation, from the constraints of everyday life, from a society which represses the self, such parties burst the bounds of middle-class entertainment and become bacchanalia. The taking of drugs is "celebrated" together,[3] a way of journeying into a realm which is completely "other", a liberating excursion from the daily round into a world of freedom and beauty. But in the background there is the number one question concerning the power of suffering and death which no freedom can resist. To avoid these questions is to inhabit a dream world, artificial and insubstantial. It takes more than emotional declamations about the suffering of oppressed peoples—which have become the stock in trade of so many of these homemade "liturgies"—to conceal their fundamental lack of grip. In other words, when "celebration" is equated with the congregation's group dynamics, when "creativity" and "ideas" are mistaken for freedom, the fact is that human nature is being soft-pedaled; its authentic reality is being bypassed. It does not take a prophet to predict that experiments of this kind will not last long; but they can result in a widespread destruction of liturgy.

Now let us turn to the positive side. We have said that liturgy is festal, and the feast is about freedom, the *freedom of being* which is there beneath the role-playing. But where we speak of being, we also raise the question of death. Therefore the festal celebration, above all else, must address itself to the question of death. Conversely, the feast presupposes joy, but this is only possible if it is able to face up to death. That is why, in the history of religions, the feast has always displayed a cosmic and universal character. It attempts to answer the question of

---

[3] Instructive details in E. K. Scheuch, *Haschisch und LSD als Modedrogen* (Osnabrück 1970).

death by establishing a connection with the universal vital power of the cosmos. At this point some may object that, if we are trying to identify what is specifically Christian, we cannot infer the nature of Christian liturgy from the manifestations of religion in general. This is quite right as far as the *positive* form and message of the Christian feast is concerned; but at the same time the fact is that the new and unique Christian reality answers the questions of *all* men. To that extent there must be a fundamental anthropological connection, otherwise what is new and specifically Christian would be unintelligible.

The novel Christian reality is this: Christ's Resurrection enables man genuinely to rejoice. All history until Christ has been a fruitless search for this joy. That is why the Christian liturgy—Eucharist—is, of its essence, the Feast of the Resurrection, *Mysterium Paschae*. As such it bears within it the mystery of the Cross, which is the inner presupposition of the Resurrection. To speak of the Eucharist as the community meal is to cheapen it, for its price was the death of Christ. And as for the joy it heralds, it presupposes that we have entered into this mystery of death. Eucharist is ordered to eschatology, and hence it is at the heart of the theology of the Cross. This is why the Church holds fast to the sacrificial character of the Mass; she does so lest we fail to realize the magnitude of what is involved and thus miss both the real depth of what it means to be human and the real depth of God's liberating power. The freedom with which we are concerned in the Christian feast—the feast of the Eucharist—is not the freedom to devise new texts but the liberation of the world and ourselves from death. Only this can make us free, enabling us to accept truth and to love one another in truth.

This basic insight automatically yields two further

structures essential to the Eucharist. One is the Eucharist's worship dimension, which is hardly mentioned in the "roles" approach. Christ died praying; his consent to his Father took precedence over political advantage, thus he was brought to the Cross. On the Cross, therefore, he held aloft his Yes to the Father, glorifying the Father in the Cross, and it was this manner of his dying which led, by an inner logic, to the Resurrection. This means that worship is the context in which we can discover joy, the liberating, victorious Yes to life. The Cross is worship, "exaltation"; Resurrection is made present in it. To celebrate the Feast of the Resurrection is to enter into worship. If we can describe the central meaning of Christian liturgy as the "Feast of the Resurrection", its formative core is "worship". In worship, death is overcome and love is made possible. Worship is truth.

Secondly, it follows that liturgy has a cosmic and universal dimension. The community does not become a community by mutual interaction. It receives its being as a gift from an already existing completeness, totality, and in return it gives itself back to this totality. We cannot go into detail here, but this is why liturgy cannot be "made". This is why it has to be simply received as a given reality and continually revitalized. This is why its universality is expressed in a form binding on the whole Church, committed to the local congregation in the form of the "rite". As "feast", liturgy goes beyond the realm of what can be made and manipulated; it introduces us to the realm of given, living reality, which communicates itself to us. That is why, at all times and in all religions, the fundamental law of liturgy has been the law of organic growth within the universality of the common tradition. Even in the huge transition from the Old to the New Testament, this rule was not breached,

the continuity of liturgical development was not inter-
rupted: Jesus introduced his words at the Last Supper
organically into the Jewish liturgy at the point where it
was open to them, as it were, waiting for them. The
growing Church carefully continued this process of
inwardly deepening, purifying and expanding the Old
Testament inheritance. Neither the apostles nor their
successors "made" a Christian liturgy; it grew organically
as a result of the Christian reading of the Jewish inheritance, fashioning its own form as it did so.[4] In this process
there was a filtering of the individual communities'
experiences of prayer, within the basic proportions of
the one Church, gradually developing into the distinctive
forms of the major regional churches. In this sense
liturgy *always* imposed an obligatory form on the
individual congregation and the individual celebrant. It
is a guarantee, testifying to the fact that something
greater is taking place here than can be brought about by
any individual community or group of people. It expresses
the gift of joy, the gift of participation in the cosmic
drama of Christ's Resurrection, by which liturgy stands
or falls. Moreover the obligatory character of the essential
parts of the liturgy also guarantees the true freedom of
the faithful: it makes sure that they are not victims of
something fabricated by an individual or a group, that
they are sharing in the same liturgy that binds the priest,
the bishop and the pope. In the liturgy, we are all given
the freedom to appropriate, in our own personal way,
the mystery which addresses us.

It is also worth observing here that the "creativity"

[4] Cf. L. Bouyer, *Eucharistie. Théologie et spiritualité de la prière
eucharistique* (Tournai 1966) [*Eucharist. Theology and Spirituality of the
Eucharistic Prayer* (London: Notre Dame, 1968)]. Cf. also in the
present work p. 85f., as well as my book (note 2 above), 34–41.

involved in manufactured liturgies has a very restricted
scope. It is poor indeed compared with the wealth of the
received liturgy in its hundreds and thousands of years of
history. Unfortunately, the originators of homemade
liturgies are slower to become aware of this than the
participants. Furthermore, those able to draw up such
liturgies are necessarily few in number, with the result
that what is "freedom" for them means "domination" as
it affects others. In the Church's received liturgy, however, there are plenty of opportunities calling for the
application of creativity. There is the artistic area,
particularly that of music; the organization of the
liturgical ministries and the preparation of the liturgical
space in ways appropriate to the particular celebration;
there is the area of the intercessions. Creativity is needed
above all in the proclamation of the word, which is
committed to the priest, where the common message is
translated into the here and now of the participants. The
man who seriously faces up to this task will be continually
and painfully aware of the limits of his "creativity": he
will hardly want further demands to be placed on it!

II. The Subjective Response to the Objective Nature of the Liturgy

So far we have tried to make plain the objective basic
structure of the liturgy, provisionally applying the concept
"feast" to it, i.e., it is the Feast of the Lord's Resurrection.
This in turn showed us the primacy of worship and the
objective motive for joy, which presupposes that the
individual and the community are bound to the universal
Church and her history as well as to the form which she
prescribes. This liturgical form is shown to be the realm

of freedom and genuine community. This naturally brings us to consider in more depth the position of the individual and the congregation in worship. As is well known, the Second Vatican Council referred to this aspect in terms of *"participatio actuosa"*, active participation. We find ourselves continually returning to this point because it is a basic problem in the theology of worship. In our present context we need to analyze the anthropological substance of this concept. Such an analysis will also be essential when it comes to a discussion of the practical measures to be taken.

In order to do justice to our humanness, "participation" and "activity" must be seen in the perspective of the individual and the community, of inwardness and external expression. For community to exist, there must be some common *expression*; but, lest this expression be merely external, there must be also a common movement of *internalization*, a shared path inward (and upward). Where man operates *only* at the level of expression, at the level of "roles", he is only "playing" at community. This "acted" community only lasts as long as the playing of the roles. We can see this in the writings of Sartre, Simone de Beauvoir and Camus. As representatives of a whole generation they have described the feeling of isolation, the sense of man's essential loneliness and the impossibility of communication between separate selves. To a large extent this lies behind the disgust with human existence which we see around us. And the feeling itself comes from the experience that the interior path only leads to the isolation of separate selves and the outer path can only cover over the total impossibility of real relationship. Christian liturgy could and should take up this very point. But it cannot do so by exhausting itself in external activity. The only way is to open up these separate selves through the process of interiorization, by an entering into the liturgical word and the liturgical reality—which is the presence of the Lord—and by enabling them inwardly to communicate with him who first communicated himself to us all, in his self-surrender on the Cross. It becomes genuinely possible for people to share in a common expression once this interiorization has taken place under the guidance of the common prayers of the Church and the experience of the Body of Christ which they contain. Then people are no longer merely juxtaposed in role-playing but actually touch one another at the level of being. Only in this way can "community" come about.

For this reason I am less than happy with the idea of liturgical "roles". Where a liturgical prayer book is used by the congregation, it certainly does enable people to fit into the common liturgical movement, and to that extent it can be seen as a "script". But it only fulfills its purpose if it enables men to stand in prayer before God in a personal way, unconcealed, stripped of "roles". Only then can we be opened up and put genuinely in touch with one another. Though it is a community prayer, the liturgy must have *real* prayer as its goal, i.e., we must speak to God, not merely to one another; then we shall be better able to speak to one another at the deepest level. This means that, in the area of liturgical participation— which is, at its most profound, a *participatio Dei*, a participation in God and hence in life and freedom—the process of interiorization is of prime importance. In turn it follows that this participation must not cease once the liturgical action is over; liturgy is not some kind of "happening", externally applied to man: it needs education and practice. Lamentably, the magnificent work done in this field by men like Romano Guardini and

Pius Parsch has been thrown into the wastepaper basket with the advent of the new books. Thank God there are signs that the inheritance bequeathed by these great liturgical teachers is being rediscovered and carried forward.[5] True liturgical formation cannot be achieved by a continual stream of new ideas and new forms. We need to be led from the form to the content. In other words, we need an education which will help us to grow into an inner appropriation of the Church's common liturgy. This is the only way to get beyond the profusion of words and explanations which tear the liturgy to pieces and ultimately explain nothing.

The question of the relationship between the individual and the community has thus brought us to the question of liturgical expression. The theology of creation and the theology of the Resurrection (which includes and ratifies Incarnation) demand that prayer should be expressed in a bodily form, involving all the dimensions of bodily expression. The spiritualization of the body calls for the embodiment of the Spirit, and vice versa. Only in this way can man and the world be "humanized", which means that matter is brought to its spiritual capacity and that the Spirit is expressed in the wealth of creation. Criticism must be applied to the one-sided dominance of the word, which is unfortunately evident even in the official liturgical books. Recently, however, there are indications that liturgical science has once again taken up the idea of sacred signs and their meaning, along the lines

[5] I see this indicated in two volumes which give a picture of the personalities and aims of two pioneers of liturgical renewal: N. Höslinger/T. Maas-Ewerd, *Mit sanfter Zähigkeit. P. Parsch und die biblisch-liturgische Erneuerung* (Klosterneuburg 1979); B. Fischer/ H. B. Meyer, *J. A. Jungmann. Ein Leben für Liturgie und Kerygma* (Innsbruck 1975).

of Romano Guardini's unforgettable little book. To liturgy belong both speech *and* silence, singing, the praise of instruments, the visual image, the symbol, and the gesture which corresponds to the word.[6]

In conclusion I would like briefly to examine two of these elements. If there is to be a real *participatio actuosa*, there must be silence. In this silence, together, we journey inward, becoming aware of word and sign, leaving behind the roles which conceal our real selves. In silence man "bides" and "abides"; he becomes aware of "abiding" reality. Liturgy's tension, tautness, does not come from "variety", as B. Kleinheyer has correctly observed,[7] but from the fact that it creates a space in which we can encounter what is truly great and inexhaustible, something that does not need "variety" because it *suffices*, namely, truth and love. If silence is of such great importance, the few seconds' pause between the "Let us pray" and the prayer itself is totally inadequate—and indeed, it often seems artificial in any case. There is scope for silence at the preparation of the gifts, as well as before and after the communion. Regrettably, the silence before Communion is very rarely observed, contrary to the intention of the Missal. I must add, though it conflicts with the accepted view, that it is not essential for the entire canon of the Mass to be recited aloud on every occasion. The idea that it *must* rests on a misunderstanding of its nature as proclamation. Where a community has

[6] Cf., e.g., J. Jorissen/H. B. Meyer, *Zeichen und Symbole im Gottesdienst* (Innsbruck 1977); B. Kleinheyer, *Heil erfahren in Zeichen* (Munich 1980). Sociology too has turned toward the symbol. Cf. M. J. Helle, *Soziologie und Symbol* (Cologne-Opladen 1969). Cf. also K. H. Bieritz, "Chancen einer ökumenischen Liturgik", in *ZKTh* 100 (1978): 470–83.

[7] B. Kleinheyer, *Erneuerung des Hochgebetes* (Regensburg 1969), 24.

undergone the requisite process of liturgical education, the congregation is well acquainted with the component parts of the Church's eucharistic prayer. In such a case it is only necessary to pray aloud the first few words of each section of the prayer—the headings, as it were; in this way the congregation's participation (and hence the quality of proclamation) will be often far greater than when its internal appropriation of the words is stifled by an uninterrupted loud recitation. The unhappy multiplication of eucharistic prayers which we see in other countries and which has long been under way here too [in Germany], is symptomatic of a very serious situation, quite apart from the fact that the quality and the theological content of some of these productions are hardly bearable. The continual recitation of the canon aloud results in the demand for "variety", but the demand is insatiable, however much these eucharistic prayers may proliferate. There is only one solution: we must address ourselves once again to the *intrinsic tension of the reality itself*. In the end even variety becomes boring. This is why, here especially, we are in such urgent need of an education toward inwardness. We need to be taught to enter into the heart of things. As far as liturgy is concerned, this is a matter of life or death. The only way we can be saved from succumbing to the inflation of words is if we have the courage to face silence and in it learn to listen afresh to the Word. Otherwise we shall be overwhelmed by "mere words" at the very point where we should be encountering *the Word*, the Logos, the Word of love, crucified and risen, who brings us life and joy.

My second observation concerns the significance of gestures. Standing, kneeling, sitting, bowing, beating one's breast, the sign of the cross—all these have an irreplaceable anthropological significance as the way the Spirit is expressed in the body. J. Pieper has shown convincingly that such gestures bring together the "outside" and the "inside" in a reciprocal relationship which is equally important for both.[8] Here I would like to refer to the gesture which is central to worship, and one which is threatening to disappear, namely, the practice of kneeling.[9] We know that the Lord knelt to pray (Lk 22:41), that Stephen (Acts 7:60), Peter (Acts 9:40) and Paul (Acts 20:36) did so too. The hymn to Christ in Philippians 2:6–11 speaks of the cosmic liturgy as a bending of the knee at the name of Jesus, seeing in it a fulfillment of the Isaian prophecy (Is 45:23) of the sovereignty of the God of Israel. In bending the knee at the name of Jesus, the Church is acting in all truth; she is entering into the cosmic gesture, paying homage to the

---

[8] J. Pieper, "Das Gedächtnis des Leibes. Von der erinnernden Kraft des Geschichtlich-Konkreten", in W. Seidel (ed.), *Kirche aus lebendigen Steinen* (Mainz 1975), 68–83.

[9] From what I have said it should be clear that those who try to hang on to a form of liturgical development which the whole Church has found obsolete are also retreating into a small-group situation; in distancing themselves from the Church's common approach, they are in fact constructing a homemade liturgy of their own. It is quite a different question whether—similarly to the reform of 1570—the Church should show her magnanimity by allowing people to continue to use the old Missal for the time being, under certain conditions. There is the further, and distinct, question as to the particular weaknesses of the new liturgical books as compared with the old, and how one might succeed in integrating some of the advantages of the old into the new. But it is of prime importance to make it clear that the real contrast is not between the old and new books but between a liturgy of the whole Church and homemade liturgies. The greatest obstacle to the calm and orderly appropriation of the renewed liturgical forms lies in the impression so often given that liturgy is now a matter of individual experiment.

Victor and thereby going over to the Victor's side. For in bending the knee we signify that we are imitating and adopting the attitude of him who, though he was "in the form of God", yet "humbled himself unto death". In this way, by combining the prophetic word of the Old Covenant and the manner of life of Jesus Christ, the Letter to the Philippians has taken up the sign of kneeling, which it regards as the appropriate posture for Christians to adopt at the name of Jesus, and has given it a cosmic significance in salvation history. Here, the bodily gesture attains the status of a confession of faith in Christ: words could not replace such a confession.

This brings us back to the concept we started with: Christian liturgy is cosmic liturgy, as Saint Paul tells us in the Letter to the Philippians. It must never renounce this dignity, however attractive it may seem to work with small groups and construct homemade liturgies. What is exciting about Christian liturgy is that it lifts us up out of our narrow sphere and lets us share in the truth. The aim of all liturgical renewal must be to bring to light this liberating greatness.[10]

---

[10] On the question of "creativity", cf. also G.-M. Oury, *La créativité liturgique* (Quebec 1977).

Part Two

Practical Applications

Change and Permanence in Liturgy

A Conversation with the Editor of the International Catholic Periodical Communio

Communio: There is no point looking for problems where there are none, so let us say at the outset that, insofar as liturgy has a form which is perceptible to the senses, it is changeable. Indeed, it must be changeable. For it is the existential presence of the celebrating, praying faithful which makes the liturgy into the worship of God; change is necessary so that their awareness of what is going on and of their part in it are not restricted by extraneous factors. Roman history reveals a most eloquent example of a form of worship which had become unintelligible. After three centuries no one any longer understood the ritual, the ceremonies or the meaning it was all meant to express, with the result that religion dried up and became an empty shell, although it was no less practiced than before. The lesson is that, if liturgy is to retain its vitality and have an influence on individuals and society, there must be a continual process of adaptation to the understanding of believers. For believers too, after all, are people of their time, people of their world.

Taking it as a fact that today, for the first time in history, the Church is really universal and encompasses the whole earth, not only in intention but *de facto*—apart from certain blank areas on the map of the Communist Far East—surely there has been far too little reform of the liturgy, of the Mass? What about the believers in mission lands? As far as they were concerned, the reform of the liturgy simply could not go far enough. Is it right that non-Western people, people with their own cultural setting, with their own and in some ways totally different symbolic forms and gestures (the embrace, bow, genuflection, kiss) should be forced into the symbols and sign language which belong to the thought and feeling of the Mediterranean world and of Europe? For it is these European forms which have shaped our liturgy.

Cardinal Ratzinger: First of all it must be said that both the Constitution on the Liturgy and the Decree on the Church's Missionary Activity explicitly allow for the possibility of far-reaching adaptations to the customs and cultic traditions of peoples. To that extent the new Missal is only providing a framework for mission lands. It is a feature of the new Missal that its very many *ad libitum* provisions give a great deal of scope for local variations. On the other hand, we must beware of seeing things too naively and simplistically. Only very slowly and with the greatest of caution did the growing Church take up certain of the external forms of pagan liturgies. At the beginning the Church operated within the form of the Jewish synagogue service—an extremely modest form from the point of view of ritual. She joined this to the celebration of the Eucharist, the basic structure of which was equally Jewish, namely, the great prayer of thanksgiving. At the core of this thanksgiving, she placed the account of the institution of the Eucharist. Hence this prayer also mediates the idea of sacrifice insofar as it is attuned to the prayer of Jesus Christ in his self-surrender to the Father and makes this self-offering present in time. These simple elements have constituted the basic structure of every Christian Eucharist right up to the present day. In the course of a gradual development they have been furnished with various cultic forms, ultimately giving rise to the individual ritual genres. But this development presupposes the existence of a Christian identity that was able to create its own fundamental liturgical form. Only on the basis of a Christian consciousness of this kind could the existing elements be refashioned in a fruitful way and made to express Christian realities. In other words, the whole process presupposes the struggle to vindicate what was distinctively Christian, a struggle carried on by the martyrs over three centuries. Only once this had been done could the door be opened to the use of pagan customs, suitably purified. Moreover, much of what we are inclined to see as adaptation from the Roman sphere of influence was in fact the product of the Old Testament renaissance which began in the early Middle Ages, i.e., here too it was far more a case of Christianity returning to appropriate its own distinct origins.

Therefore it seems to me very dangerous to suggest that missionary liturgies could be created overnight, so to speak, by decisions of Bishops' Conferences, which would themselves be dependent on memoranda drawn up by academics. Liturgy does not come about through regulation. One of the weaknesses of the postconciliar liturgical reform can doubtless be traced to the armchair strategy of academics, drawing up things on paper which, in fact, would presuppose years of organic growth. The most blatant example of this is the reform of the Calendar: those responsible simply did not realize how much the various annual feasts had influenced Christian people's relation to time. In redistributing these established feasts throughout the year according to some historical arithmetic—inconsistently applied at that—they ignored a fundamental law of religious life. But to return to the missionary situation: conversion to Christianity means, initially, turning away from pagan forms of life. There was a very clear awareness of this in the first Christian centuries, even long after the so-called Constantinian settlement. Not until a strong Christian identity has grown up in the mission countries can one begin to move, with great caution and on the basis of this identity, toward christening the indigenous forms by adopting them into the liturgy and allowing Christian realities to merge with the forms of everyday life. It goes without saying that expressions which have no meaning in a particular country, or which have a contrary meaning, have been altered. I would not call this liturgical "reform", however, but the appropriate application of the existing form, something which is always necessary. What is more, I am convinced that a superficial or overhasty adaptation, far from attracting respect for Christianity, would only raise doubts as to its sincerity and the serious-ness of its message. Then, too, we must remember that nowadays all indigenous cultures are overlaid by features of the technological world civilization, a fact which should caution us against haste and too much attention to externals.

Communio: I am sure you share my opinion that no reform can be meaningful unless it finds wide support. Otherwise it will fail to reach its goal. We see something similar in the field of law. A new law, unobjectionable in itself, will be useless if people do not understand it and do not accept it. In such a case jurists speak of a *lex non accepta*. Having followed the debate about the reform of the liturgy, i.e., of the Mass, which has been going on in recent years both here and abroad, I would like tentatively to suggest this: though small in numbers, there seems to be a definite stratum of the faithful, very committed in their Church membership, whose response to the reform ranges from surprise, puzzlement, discontent, right up to informal and even public protest. Perhaps Church leaders think "Let them be; the protests will die down eventually." I do not want to go into all the reasons adduced against the reform. But one thing is certain: the so-called "conservatives" who form this opposition, for whatever reason, feel that they have been betrayed and put in the wrong. Nor is this a wholly subjective matter. For instance, in 1947 we had *Mediator Dei*, the encyclical of Pius XII, and then, not twenty years later, came the reform. In other words, within twenty years a silent landslide took place, without the slightest assurance being given to those involved, the mass of traditional believers. I find it hard to understand how the Church could have so failed to carry out her pastoral responsibilities toward those under her care, leaving the believers of the old school almost defenseless against the tide of new thought and practice.

The people I am referring to had been taught certain things, had been brought up in a certain way. They had fought for these values. They had been committed to them. Now, overnight, all this was no longer supposed to be true. I am not so much interested in what is right and wrong here, the old belief or the new, but I do want to point out the situation as it appears in the minds of many of the faithful.

Cardinal Ratzinger: First of all I must take up the distinction you have just made between "the old belief" and "the new". I must emphatically deny such a distinction. The Council has not created any new matter for belief, let alone replaced an old belief with a new one.

Fundamentally, the Council sees itself as continuing and deepening the work of earlier councils, in particular those of Trent and Vatican I. Its sole concern is to facilitate the same faith under changed circumstances, to revitalize it. That is why the reform of the liturgy aimed at making the faith's expression more transparent. But what we have is a renewed expression of the one faith, not a change in faith.

As to what led up to the reform: there seemed to be more going on in Germany, in terms of preparatory work, than anywhere else. Germany was the heartland of the liturgical movement, which had a great impact on the declarations of the Council. Many of the measures taken by the Council had long been anticipated here. Moreover, Pius XII had already carried out certain elements of liturgical reform—one thinks of the refashioning of the Easter Vigil. All the same I must admit that in the wake of the Council a lot of things happened far too quickly and abruptly, with the result that many of the faithful could not see the inner continuity with what had gone before. In part it is simply a fact that the Council was pushed aside. For instance, it had said that the language of the Latin Rite was to remain Latin, although suitable scope was to be given to the vernacular. Today we might ask: *Is* there a Latin Rite at all any more? Certainly there is no awareness of it. To most people the liturgy seems to be rather something for the individual congregation to arrange. Core groups make up their own "liturgies" from week to week, with an enthusiasm which is as amazing as it is misplaced. The really serious thing, in my view, is this fundamental breakdown of liturgical consciousness. Imperceptibly, the distinctions between liturgy and conviviality, liturgy and society, become blurred. Thus many priests, following the etiquette of polite society, feel that they must not receive

Communion until all the others have been "served"; or they no longer feel able to say "I bless *you*" and so dissolve the basic liturgical relationship between priest and people. Here too is the origin of all those tasteless and banal forms of greeting—which many congregations endure with polite stoicism. In the period before the appearance of the new Missal, when the old Missal was already stigmatized as antiquated, there was a loss of the awareness of "rite", i.e., that there is a prescribed liturgical form and that liturgy can only be liturgy to the extent that it is beyond the manipulation of those who celebrate it. Even the official new books, which are excellent in many ways, occasionally show far too many signs of being drawn up by academics and reinforce the notion that a liturgical book can be "made" like any other book.

In this connection I would like to make a brief reference to the so-called Tridentine liturgy. In fact there is no such thing as a Tridentine liturgy, and until 1965 the phrase would have meant nothing to anyone. The Council of Trent did not "make" a liturgy. Strictly speaking, there is no such thing, either, as the Missal of Pius V. The Missal which appeared in 1570 by order of Pius V differed only in tiny details from the first printed edition of the Roman Missal of about a hundred years earlier. Basically the reform of Pius V was only concerned with eliminating certain late medieval accretions and the various mistakes and misprints which had crept in. Thus, again, it prescribed the Missal of the City of Rome, which had remained largely free of these blemishes, for the whole Church. At the same time it was felt that if the *Missale typicum* printed in Rome were used exclusively, it would help to get rid of the uncertainties which had arisen in the confusion of liturgical movements in the Reformation period, for in this liturgical confusion the distinction between Catholic and Reformed had been widely obscured. This is clear from the fact that the reform explicitly made an exception of those liturgical customs which were more than two hundred years old. In 1614, under Urban VIII, there was already a new edition of the Missal, again including various improvements. In this way each century before and after Pius V left its mark on the Missal. On the one hand, it was subject to a continuous process of purification, and on the other, it continued to grow and develop, but it remained the same book throughout. Hence those who cling to the "Tridentine Missal" have a faulty view of the historical facts. Yet at the same time, the way in which the renewed Missal was presented is open to much criticism. We must say to the "Tridentines" that the Church's liturgy is alive, like the Church herself, and is thus always involved in a process of maturing which exhibits greater and lesser changes. Four hundred years is far too young an age for the Catholic liturgy—because in fact it reaches right back to Christ and the apostles and has come down to us from that time in a single, constant process. The Missal can no more be mummified than the Church herself. Yet, with all its advantages, the new Missal was published as if it were a book put together by professors, not a phase in a continual growth process. Such a thing has never happened before. It is absolutely contrary to the laws of liturgical growth, and it has resulted in the nonsensical notion that Trent and Pius V had "produced" a Missal four hundred years ago. The Catholic liturgy was thus reduced to the level of a mere product of modern times. This loss of perspective is really disturbing. Although very few of those who express their uneasiness have a clear picture of these interrelated factors, there is an instinctive grasp of the fact that liturgy cannot be the result of Church regulations, let alone professional erudition, but, to be true to itself, must be the fruit of the Church's life and vitality.

Lest there be any misunderstanding, let me add that as far as its content is concerned (apart from a few criticisms), I am very grateful for the new Missal, for the way it has enriched the treasury of prayers and prefaces, for the new eucharistic prayers and the increased number of texts for use on weekdays, etc., quite apart from the availability of the vernacular. But I do regard it as unfortunate that we have been presented with the idea of a new book rather than with that of continuity within a single liturgical history. In my view, a new edition will need to make it quite clear that the so-called Missal of Paul VI is nothing other than a renewed form of the same Missal to which Pius X, Urban VIII, Pius V and their predecessors have contributed, right from the Church's earliest history. It is of the very essence of the Church that she should be aware of her unbroken continuity throughout the history of faith, expressed in an ever-present unity of prayer. This awareness of continuity is destroyed just as much by those who "opt" for a book supposed to have been produced four hundred years ago as by those who would like to be forever drawing up new liturgies. At bottom, these two attitudes are identical. It seems to me that this is the origin of the uneasiness to which you have referred. The fundamental issue is whether faith comes about through regulations and learned research or through the living history of a Church which retains her identity throughout the centuries.

Communio: Going on from the question of the method applied in the reform and the effects it had, perhaps we may ask about its *aims*. As early as *Mediator Dei* we find references to the active participation of the faithful in worship. What is meant by this active participation? Singing and praying together, responding to the priest? Sitting, standing, kneeling? In other words, it is not enough to be simply present in the church, as one could before the First World War, listening to the music of the choir or praying the Rosary at Mass. Now, surely, with the whole congregation, we need to be involved in what is going on at the altar.

But is it not true to say that there already was this kind of active participation, at least in Germany, before the Second World War, thanks to the liturgical movement of the twenties? And long experience has shown us, surely, that active participation, understood in this way, can itself become an empty form. I can sing "Holy God we praise thy name" or Credo III and at the same time be going over the details of my last income tax return. Active participation is no guarantee against the dangers of routine. The question is how to preserve and create a sense of freshness and uniqueness on each occasion. What kind of active participation can help us to do this?

Cardinal Ratzinger: Perhaps I can begin by saying something about the idea of *participatio actuosa*—"active participation"—which is indeed a key phrase in the Constitution on the Liturgy of Vatican II. What lies behind it is the awareness that Christian liturgy, of its very nature, is something performed in the context of a community. It involves prayer dialogues, greetings, proclamation, praying together. People are referred to as "we" and "you"; the "I" occurs in only a few relatively late prayers. Here we are involved in an action, a "drama", in which we all play our part. This being so, the liturgical celebration, from its very structure, calls

for the interplay of words and acts between the participants. Otherwise there would arise an inner conflict
between the text and what actually takes place. This was
the discovery made by the liturgical movement, and it
gave a new immediacy to the old words and gestures. At
this point the Council was simply lending its authority
to something which was self-evident. Generally speaking,
this insight proved most fruitful. If one were to remove
the active involvement which exists in today's liturgy—
and the Council facilitated this involvement—it would
immediately be obvious how much growth there has
been. No one would want to be without it. But it is
always possible for any true insight to be diminished,
interpreted one-sidedly or distorted. Many protagonists
of liturgical reform seemed to think that if we only did
everything together and in a loud voice, the liturgy
would automatically become attractive and effective.
They forgot that the spoken words also have a *meaning*,
and part of *participatio actuosa* is to carry out that meaning.
They failed to notice that the *actio* does not consist only
or primarily in the alternation of standing, sitting and
kneeling, but in inner processes. It is these which give
rise to the whole drama of the liturgy. "Let us pray"—
this is an invitation to share in a movement which
reaches down into our inner depths. "Lift up your
hearts"—this phrase and the movement which accom-
panies it are, so to speak, only the "tip of the iceberg".
The real action takes place in the deep places of men's
hearts, which are lifted up to the heights. "Behold the
Lamb of God"—here we have an invitation to a special
kind of beholding, at a much deeper level than the
external beholding of the Host. Where this inner dimension was neglected, the liturgy still seemed "boring" and
"unintelligible", with the result that ultimately the Bible

was replaced by Marx and the sacrament by a kind of
"party" atmosphere. People wanted to "turn on" an
immediate effect, as it were, from outside. Compared
with the merely external busy-ness which became the
rule in many places, the quiet "following" of Mass, as
we knew it in former times, was far more realistic and
dramatic: it was a sharing in the action at a deep level,
and in it the community of faith was silently and power-
fully mobilized. Of course, to say this is not to impugn
"active participation" as I have defined it; the criticism
only applies where this participation has degenerated
into mere externals. There is simply no way of ensuring
that everyone, always and on all occasions, is involved in
the *actio*. Indeed, I think it is one of the crucial insights
we have gained in the wake of the Council that the
liturgy's effect cannot be achieved in a purely external
manner. Faith requires a continual process of education,
otherwise the words of faith begin to lose their meaning.
In the Gospel, immediately after the first occurrence of a
confession of faith in Christ, we read "he began to teach
them" (Mk 8:29ff.). In other words, there is no such
thing as a self-explanatory short formula of faith. The
Creed is part of an organic context which includes
teaching, education and the life of a believing fellowship;
both words and signs draw their life from this context.

Communio: I would like to ask you about the relationship
between form and content in the celebration of Mass
today. By content I have in mind the mysteries of faith
represented by and through the Church. No experienced
observer can fail to notice the change of emphasis in the
Eucharist between the meal element, the sacrificial
element and the liturgy of the word. I am stating a fact,
not making a judgment. No doubt the liturgy of the

word has gained immeasurably as a result. But the question remains: Why this change of emphasis? Obviously it was not for some merely pragmatic reason, as if something had to be cut to make room for the extended liturgy of the word.

Let me give you my hypothesis: as long as there is no consensus with regard to the content of the celebration, there will be something wrong with the form and structure which manifest this content. What is the Mass? Is it a table fellowship? Or a sacrificial fellowship? You have given your answer on pages 33–60 of this book. But I want to press you further: Is the Mass about the Real Presence of him who died on the Cross and was raised, or is it about symbols which speak of this mystery and are maybe surrogates for it? Moreover, do the ideas of transsignification and transfinalization do away with the doctrine of transubstantiation? The theologian cannot have it both ways. What are the realities involved? Is it the faith of the believers which causes the host to become the Body and Blood of Christ? Or does it become so only by being eaten—the *ut sumatur* of Saint Thomas? And if we assume that such a view of the Eucharist has a place within the Church, do we need a priest with the power to consecrate? Cannot a faithful layman do it just as well? And what about the Consecration rite? Does it not detract from the mystery, does it not destroy the symbolism and open the door to ideas of magic and miracle? Such questions are not new to you. Where the sacrificial character of the Mass is concerned, it is all too easy to ask pointed questions. In 1966 Paul VI, in his encyclical *Mysterium Fidei*, still saw the sacrificial element as the core of the eucharistic mystery. The same applies to the eucharistic cult. All the questions I have touched on are in a state of flux. No doubt the theologians will say that the Real Presence and transubstantiation are quite safe; they are simply bearing a different emphasis. I am saying that they are being *differently interpreted*. Again, I am not so much concerned with the rights and wrongs of all these questions. The issue before us is "Change and Permanence in Liturgy" with reference to the celebration of the Eucharist. On the basis of the facts, we cannot exclude the possibility—without changing the premise that in and through the Mass the faithful serve and worship God, which is always true, of course—that there has been a greater change in the understanding of the Eucharist than its nature, the understanding of its origins and the received faith of the Church permit.

Cardinal Ratzinger: The very many questions you have raised on this fourth point are so deeply involved with central dogmatic issues that it would be impossible to take them up within the space of this interview. One would need to undertake a substantial piece of catechesis. Here, a few remarks will have to suffice. I will begin with a single detail which has wider implications. The *ut sumatur* ("so that it may be consumed") which you quoted comes in fact from the Council of Trent (DS 1643); Karl Rahner pointed out that it is to be found there, in the chapter which concerns eucharistic adoration and Corpus Christi. Rahner's intention was to remind us that Trent too had a very clear view of the words of institution and the inner finality of the realities of bread and wine, asserting that it is of the essence of this sacrament (and *mutatis mutandis* of all sacraments) that it is ordered to *reception*. But this awareness did not stop Trent going on to say that this "reception" encompasses many factors: to "receive" Christ essentially involves "adoration". Receiving Christ must involve all the dimensions of Christ; so it cannot be

limited to a physical process. It also implies belief in the
Real Presence. It is so hard to define this adequately
because nowadays we no longer have a philosophy which
penetrates to the being of things. We are only interested
in function. Modern science only asks "How does it
work? What can I do with it?" It no longer asks "What
is it?"; such a question would be regarded as unscientific,
and indeed, in a strictly scientific sense, it is insoluble.
The attempts to define the Eucharist by reference to the
level of meaning and the goal (transsignification, transfinalization) were intended as a response to this new
situation. Although these new concepts are not simply
wrong, they are dangerously limited. Once sacraments
and faith are reduced to the level of function, we are no
longer speaking of God (for he is not a "function"), nor
are we speaking of man either (for he is not a function,
although he *has* many functions). Here we can see
how important it is, in a philosophically impoverished
era, for sacramental faith to keep alive the question
of being. This is the only way to break up the tyranny
of functionalism, which would turn the world into one
vast concentration camp. When nowadays we affirm
that Christ is present at the level of being in the transformed gifts, we are doing something which, up to a
point, is not backed up or "covered" by philosophy;
therefore the affirmation becomes all the more significant
as a human act.

On the relationship of the sacrifice and meal elements,
I can only refer you back to the section on "Form and
Content in the Eucharistic Celebration". But I will say
this: modern theology is rather against drawing parallels
between the history of religions and Christianity. All the
same I regard it as significant that, throughout the entire
history of religions, sacrifice and meal are inseparably

united. The sacrifice facilitates *communio* with the divinity, and men receive back the divinity's gift in and from the sacrifice. This is transformed and deepened in many ways in the mystery of Jesus Christ: here the sacrifice itself comes from the incarnate love of God, so that it is God who *gives himself*, taking man up into his action and enabling him to be both gift and recipient. Perhaps I can illustrate what I mean here by taking up another small detail: you raised the question "Do we need a priest with the power to consecrate?" I would prefer not to speak of "power", although this term has been used since the early Middle Ages. I think it is better to approach it from another angle. In order that what happened *then* may become present *now*, the words "This is my body—this is my blood" must be said. But the speaker of these words is the "I" of Jesus Christ. Only he can say them; they are *his* words. No man can dare to take to himself the "I" and "my" of Jesus Christ—and yet the words must be said if the saving mystery is not to remain something in the distant past. So authority to pronounce them is needed, an authority which no one can assume and which no congregation, nor even many congregations together, can confer. Only Jesus Christ himself, in the "sacramental" form he has committed to the whole Church, can give this authority. The word must be located, as it were, in sacrament; it must be part of the "sacrament" of the Church, partaking of an authority which she does not create, but only transmits. This is what is meant by "ordination" and "priesthood". Once this is understood, it becomes clear that, in the Church's Eucharist, something is happening which goes far beyond any human celebration, any human joint activity, and any liturgical efforts on the part of a particular community. What is taking place is the mystery of God, communicated to us by Jesus Christ through his death and Resurrection. This is what makes the Eucharist irreplaceable; this is the guarantee of its identity. The reform has not altered it: its aim was simply to shed new light upon it.

On the Theological Basis of Church Music

Introduction: Some Aspects of the Postconciliar Dispute with Regard to Church Music

It is astonishing to find that in the German edition of the documents of Vatican II, edited by Karl Rahner and Herbert Vorgrimler, the brief commentary which introduces the chapter on Sacred Music in the Constitution on the Liturgy begins with the observation that genuine art, as found in church music, is "of its very nature—which is esoteric in the best sense—hardly to be reconciled with the nature of the liturgy and the basic principle of liturgical reform".[1] It is astonishing, because the Constitution on the Liturgy, on which it is supposed to be commenting, does not see music as "merely an addition and ornamentation of the liturgy" but as itself liturgy, an integrating part of the complete liturgical action.[2] Of course neither Rahner nor Vorgrimler want to banish all music from the worship of God; but what they do find alien to its nature is art music, i.e., the musical heritage of the Western Church. Consequently they feel that the Council, in recommending that "the treasury of sacred music is to be preserved and cultivated with great care",[3] does not mean "that this is to be done within

[1] K. Rahner/H. Vorgrimler, *Kleines Konzilskompendium*, 2nd ed. (Freiburg 1967), 48.

[2] Cf. J. A. Jungmann, in *Das zweite Vatikanische Konzil. Dokumente und Kommentare I* (= *LThK* Supplement I), 95f.

[3] Constitution on the Sacred Liturgy, chap. 6, art. 114.

the framework of the liturgy".[4] In a similar vein our commentators lay stress on the Council's recommendation that choirs should be cultivated "especially in cathedral churches", and in context the impression is given that the Council really wanted to limit them to cathedrals, and even then provided they did not obstruct the people's participation.[5] For Rahner and Vorgrimler, the normal musical component of liturgy is hence not "actual church music" but "so-called utility music".[6]

Now we can grant the fact that there is a definite tension within the Council document; it reflects the tension between the various approaches represented in the Council itself, but it may also reflect a tension inherent in the subject. This document contains a very clear recommendation of what Rahner and Vorgrimler call "actual church music": in addition to what we have already seen, there is particular emphasis on the teaching of church music in seminaries and on the training of church musicians and singers, especially boys. Special mention is made of the desirability of establishing "higher institutes of sacred music".[7] Gregorian chant is particularly recommended, but there is also an express affirmation of polyphony.[8] There is also a positively enthusiastic

[4] See note 1 above.

[5] See note 1 above; cf. Constitution on the Sacred Liturgy, art. 114: "The treasury of sacred music is to be preserved and cultivated with great care. Choirs must be assiduously developed, especially in cathedral churches. Bishops and other pastors of souls must take great care to ensure that whenever the sacred action is to be accompanied by chant, the whole body of the faithful may be able to contribute that active participation which is rightly theirs . . ." *Vatican Council II. The Conciliar and Post Conciliar Documents*, ed. A. Flannery (Dublin 1975).

[6] See note 1 above.

[7] Cf. Constitution on the Sacred Liturgy, art. 115.

[8] Art. 116.

panegyric upon the pipe organ, causing J. A. Jungmann to remark that this most ancient instrument of church music is praised here in terms "markedly different from the usually sober, juridical language".[9] But other instruments too are encouraged in church music, under the conditions formulated by tradition.[10] On the other hand, we must acknowledge that, together with the affirmation of this rich inheritance with its high technical demands, there is a desire to see the liturgy completely open to all, a desire for the common participation of all in the liturgical action, including liturgical singing, and this, inevitably, must put a curb on artistic requirements.

Comparing the Council document itself with the commentary by Rahner and Vorgrimler, we find a contrast which is characteristic of the difference, in general, between what the Council said and how it has been taken up by the postconciliar Church. During the Council the Fathers became aware of a problem which had not arisen in such a pointed form before—the tension between the demands of art and the simplicity of the liturgy; but when experts and pastors meet together, the pastoral issues predominate, with the result that the view of the whole starts to get out of focus. In its struggle for unanimity, the Council document maintains a difficult balance; what happens then is that it is read one-sidedly in the interests of a particular concern, and the original balance becomes a useful rule of thumb: the liturgy needs utility music, and "actual church music" must be cultivated elsewhere—it is no longer suitable for the liturgy. People are prepared to overlook the fact that, in this view, "actual church music" is no longer actually music for the Church, that the Church no longer has "actual

---

[9] See note 2 above, p. 99; also art. 120 of the Constitution.
[10] Art. 120.

church music". The years which followed witnessed the increasingly grim impoverishment which follows when beauty for its own sake is banished from the Church and all is subordinated to the principle of "utility". One shudders at the lackluster face of the postconciliar liturgy as it has become, or one is bored with its banality and its lack of artistic standards; all the same, this development has at least created a situation in which one can begin to ask questions.

So let us take up this problem: genuine art is "esoteric in the best sense", say Rahner and Vorgrimler; liturgy is simple; it must be possible for everyone, particularly the simple, to participate. Can liturgy accommodate real church music? Does it in fact demand it, or does it exclude it? In looking for an answer to these questions, we will not find much help in our theological inheritance. It seems that relations between theology and church music have always been somewhat cool. Yet if there is to be a meaningful answer, it must lie within historical Christian experience, i.e., within the compass of tradition; for this is where the problem is worked over, this is where we discover the response to issues at stake and a view of liturgy and of church music as they have developed throughout a common history.

There can be no doubt that these problems have been seen differently over the course of time. With Rahner and Vorgrimler the issue is that of the "esoteric" versus "utility", and they opt for the latter. It would probably be a mistake to look for some deep philosophical factor behind this attitude; largely it is the average pastoral reaction, recalling the perennial dispute between the pragmatic, practical man and the specialist. Certainly there are underlying attitudes at work here: the Baroque period with its manifest delight in music was succeeded

by the Enlightenment's pedagogic interest, its concern
with rationality and reason; the Cecilian movement was
followed by the liturgical movement, initially exaggera-
ting the importance of Gregorian chant, which appealed
to the romantic nostalgia characteristic of large parts of
the movement; then came the craze for utility, for the
catchy melody, for the participation of everyone in everything. A related factor may be seen in the way modern
art has taken refuge more and more in specialism, in the
high pitch of virtuosity, in the abstruse and abstract,
leaving nothing but schmaltz for the general public. It
may also be symptomatic of the divisive tendency of the
present age: its rationalism has erected the dilemma of
specialism versus banality, while its functionalism ruins
any sense of the integrity and vitality, the wholeness, of
the artistic utterance. Ultimately it goes back to a conception of activity, community and equality which no
longer knows the unity-creating power of shared listening,
shared wonder, the shared experience of being moved at
a level deeper than words. At all events, one thing has
become clear in recent years: the retreat into utility has
not made the liturgy more open; it has only impoverished
it. This is not the way to create the required simplicity.

Church Music as a Theological Problem in the Work
Of Thomas Aquinas and in the Authorities He Cites

As we have already said, the antithesis of the esoteric
versus utility formulated by Rahner and Vorgrimler is
only a contemporary variation of a problem which goes
back to the dawn of Christianity. If we are to get to the
bottom of it, we must at least take a look at another,
earlier form of the same problem. Some years ago

W. Kurzschenkel produced a historical treatment of music in theology; but while it did open up our present topic, it by no means presented a complete answer.[11] Here I would like to give a glimpse of the debate in history by analyzing the relevant *quaestiones* of Saint Thomas Aquinas. This will be particularly valuable because it is part of the greatness of his work that it mirrors all the substantial elements of tradition. Thomas discusses the question in his analysis of the concept and nature of "religio", by which he does not mean "religion" in the modern sense but the whole context of the cult, of the worship of God.[12] Here *one* question is devoted to the problem of "the praise of God with the external voice". The introductory article asks whether the vocal praise of God is meaningful at all, and a second article enquires "whether singing can be brought into the praise of God".[13] Now the Church has been singing since the time of Jesus and the apostles, for they sang in the synagogue and brought that singing into the Church.[14]

[11] W. Kurzschenkel, *Die theologische Bestimmung der Musik* (Trier 1971). Important material also in K. G. Fellerer (ed.), *Geschichte der katholischen Kirchenmusik* (Kassel, 1: 1972; 2: 1976); quoted in what follows as Fellerer, *Geschichte* (all references to volume 1).

[12] Cf. H. J. Burbach, *Studien zur Musikanschauung des Thomas von Aquin* (Regensburg 1966); id., "Thomas von Aquin und die Musik", in *Musica sacra* 94 (1974): 80–82. There is an analysis of Thomas' treatise on worship in E. Heck, *Der Begriff religio bei Thomas von Aquin* (Paderborn 1971). A useful commentary on questions 81–200 of the *Summa* 2a–2ae is that of F. Mennessier, *St. Thomas d'Aquin, La Religion*, 1 and 2 (Paris 1953).

[13] *Summa* 2a–2ae q 91 a 1 and 2, Mennessier 2: 136–48; commentary, 391–93. A full, though in my view too subjective, interpretation of this text is found in D. Sertillanges, "Prière et Musique", in *Vie Intellectuelle* 7 (1930): 130–64.

[14] Cf. K. G. Fellerer, "Die katholische Kirchenmusik in Geschichte und Gegenwart", in Fellerer, *Geschichte*, 1ff., esp. 1: "The great Hallel (Ps 113–18) at the Last Supper (Mt 26:30; Mk 14:26) signifies the

To that extent the principle is established. All the same, weighty arguments were adduced, not against singing entirely, but for limiting it very severely, by those people whose conception of the nature of Christianity allowed only a restricted significance to singing in church.

1. *Theology's* Auctoritates *Question*
The Value of Church Music

Thomas was confronted primarily with three influential traditional authorities critical of church music. Two of these had gained admission into the "Decretum" of Gratian and had thus more or less acquired the status of customary law. First there is the somewhat coarse asceticism of Jerome, which Gratian had adopted into his handbook. Commenting on the words in Ephesians which speak of Christians singing hymns and psalms to God in their hearts (5:19), he wrote: "This applies particularly to the young people who perform the ministry of psalmist in the church: they should sing to God with their hearts, not with their voices, not plastering neck and throat with ointments like stage-players, churning out theatrical tunes and songs in church."[15] Whatever one thinks of this outburst of the controversial exegete, it is clear that at his time there was an artistically developed church music.

---

beginning of Christian cultic song." For an extremely instructive article, cf. Eric Werner, "Die jüdischen Wurzeln der christlichen Kirchenmusik", ibid., 22–30, esp. 26.

[15] *Comm in ep ad Eph* III 5, PL 26:528 C–D; *Decr. Gratiani* I dist. 92 c 1; Thomas Aquinas, 2a–2ae 1 91 a 2 opp.2. The passage is quoted in H. Hüschen, "Musik der 'Anbetung im Geiste' ", in Fellerer, *Geschichte*, 36. I follow Hüschen in translating the (technical) term "moduli" as "tunes" ("melodies").

Next to Jerome there is Pope Gregory the Great. In the context of a local Roman synod he prohibited clerics, once they had been ordained to the diaconate, from functioning as cantors (and even added an anathema to the decree), lest they should be distracted from their proper task, namely, the proclamation of the word and the service of the poor. Moreover, Gregory is aware of moral danger too: a fateful contradiction could easily develop between the beautiful voice and the manner of life, between the admiration of the listeners and the verdict of God. So the higher clergy must restrict their musical activity to the singing of the Gospel at Mass; all other musical tasks—the singing of the psalms and the other readings—are to be performed by the lower clergy, by subdeacons or, in case of necessity, by those in minor orders.[16] Evidently, fanatics found support in this canon for their enmity toward church music. But the most important argument comes from the tradition of interpretation of the New Testament itself, which we have already seen in a particularly angular form in Jerome. Colossians 3:16 speaks of praising God with "spiritual songs", and exegesis generally took this as a clear authority for the maxim *"Deus mente colitur magis quam ore"*—God is honored more by the spirit than by the mouth.[17]

Finally we should note an observation which Thomas makes almost as an aside: "In the praise of God the Church does not employ musical instruments . . . lest it appear to be falling back into Jewish ways."[18] Instrumental music, understood as a "judaizing element",

[16] Gratian, *Decr.* I d 92 c 2; Thomas q 91 a 2 opp.3; cf. PL 77:1335 A–B (Appendix, V *Decreta sancti Gregorii Papae I*).

[17] Q 91 a 1 opp.2. Cf. the detailed presentation of this line of tradition in H. Hüschen, op. cit., 31–36.

[18] Q 91 a 2 opp.4. Thomas would probably have made use of the eighth book of Aristotle's *Politics* to go into this question more

simply disappeared from the liturgy without any discussion; the instrumental music of the Jewish Temple is
dismissed as a mere concession to the hardness of heart
and sensuality of the people at the time. What the Old
Testament said about music in worship could no longer
be applied directly; it had to be read allegorically, it had
to be spiritualized. Thomas could not have known that,
precisely by banning instrumental music and severely
restricting church music to the vocal sphere, the Church
was expressing her continuity with early Judaism,
linking up with the musical practice of the synagogue
and also with the puritanism of the Pharisees, who
utterly discountenanced instrumental music.[19] As far as
the Church was concerned, the decision had a certain
consistency since there was no direct connection with
the Temple worship; the liturgy of the Church could
only be developed initially along the lines of synagogue
worship, not of the Temple cult. In Thomas (or rather in
the tradition received by him), this practical reason does
in fact acquire the status of a principle: instrumental
music is put under the category of "the law", which is
not to be understood literally but spiritually. Thus the
problem of church music is seen as part of the problem
of law and gospel. In the patristic, Platonic tradition of

deeply, but unfortunately he did not write the commentary on this
book which is attributed to him. In fact the latter was written by his
pupil Peter of Auvergne (cf. H. J. Burbach, op. cit., 14) and restricts
itself to a paraphrase of the text without dealing with the problem. In
his commentary on Psalm 32:2, Thomas does attempt to adapt
Aristotle's political approach to music to the new musical situation
created by the medieval Church but without taking into account the
changed significance of the modes (Doric—Phrygian—and, as he
calls it, "Hippolydian"), with the result that the problem is not
substantially advanced. Cf. H. J. Burbach, op. cit., 50–58; Mennessier,
393; on Aristotle in the present study, see notes 27 and 44 below.

[19] Cf. E. Werner, op. cit. (see note 14), 25ff.

exegesis, the opposition of law and gospel is largely identified with the philosophical opposition of the sensual and the spiritual; in concrete terms this means that music (and particularly instrumental music) falls under the heading of the sensual; the "spiritual" movement of the gospel must therefore be seen more or less as the renunciation of the sensual reality of musical sound in favor of the solely spiritual, i.e., the word alone.

2. Issues Underlying the Theological Critique of Music

Thus we have already gone beyond the question of "authorities" to consider intrinsic reasons, and this will enable us to assess the meaning and scope of the positive theology of church music which Aquinas erects in order to counter the negative position of the traditional authorities. Analyzing the texts—not infrequent in the Fathers—which are critical of music or even openly hostile to it, one can clearly identify two constant and governing factors:

a. In the first place there is a one-sidedly "spiritual" understanding of the relationship between the Old and New Testaments, between law and gospel. It is a fact that, in the transition from Israel to the Gentile Church, a highly influential part was played (in terms of the preparation of a climate of thought) by the spiritual currents which had long been a medium for the encounter of Jewish faith and philosophical piety. This philosophical piety had enabled Greek thought to abandon polytheism and its cults; in its monotheistic yearnings and its interiority it could influence and combine with the Jewish spirit. For its part, the Jewish diaspora had been obliged to ask serious questions about its own universal form, and even in Palestine itself, with the increasing importance of the synagogue and the advance of ideas critical of the Temple, there was a strong tendency toward spiritualizing its historical inheritance of faith.[20] No doubt it is this spiritualizing tendency which lies behind the "allegory" in which Paul expressed the freedom from law (Gal 4:24); for Paul, to read the Old Testament with a view to Christ is to read it in a "spiritual" sense.[21] All the same, to christianize the Old Testament is not simply to spiritualize it: it also implies incarnation.[22] In principle the Church Fathers were aware of this; the fight against gnosticism, as that against Arius, is a fight against a merely "spiritual" understanding of Christianity which would have changed it from a concrete faith into a religious philosophy.

[20] Cf. the material in C. K. Barrett, *The New Testament Background: Selected Documents* (London 1956). A survey of the Jewish area is available in M. Simon, *Die jüdischen Sekten zur Zeit Christi* (Einsiedeln 1964); on the whole problem, cf. also H. A. Wolfson, *The Philosophy of the Church Fathers*, I (Cambridge, Mass. 1956); O. Gigon, *Die antike Kultur und das Christentum* (Gütersloh 1966), and the wealth of material in Hüschen, op. cit., 31–36.

[21] Cf. H. de Lubac, *Exegèse mediévale, les quatre sens de l'Écriture* (Paris 1959, 1960); also id., *Histoire et Esprit, l'intelligence de l'Écriture d'après Origène* (Paris 1950). On Thomas' handling of the issue: M. Arias-Reyero, *Thomas von Aquin als Exeget* (Einsiedeln 1971). See also my remarks in Internat. Theologenkommission, *Die Einheit des Glaubens und der theologische Pluralismus* (Einsiedeln 1973), 22–29.

[22] Internat. Theologenkommission, op. cit., 26, with further refs. I am not entirely satisfied with the otherwise valuable book by T. Maertens, *Heidnisch-jüdische Wurzeln der christlichen Feste* (Mainz 1965) [*A Feast in honor of Yahweh* (Notre Dame, Ind. 1965)], since it puts forward the "spiritualization" view one-sidedly. By contrast, the specifically Christian perspective is very well demonstrated in J. Daniélou, *The Bible and the Liturgy* (London 1956).

In retrospect it must be said, however, that the Fathers could not simply step out of the intellectual climate of their time; they were obliged to make concessions to it which went beyond what was permissible and appropriate from the point of view of Christianity. Once again we must assert that there is and can be a genuine communion of interest between Christianity and Platonism. The "allegory" of the Old Testament, on which Christianity is founded, is closely related to the "allegory" which arises from Platonic thought; or rather, put more exactly: as spiritual paths, Christianity and Platonism pursue parallel courses for quite a distance. But in Christian terms, "spiritualization" is not simply opposition to the world of the senses, as in Platonic mysticism, but a drawing near to the Lord who "is the Spirit" (2 Cor 3:17; cf. 1 Cor 15:45). Therefore the body is included in this spiritualization: the Lord is "the Spirit" precisely in that his body does not experience corruption (Ps 15:9f. LXX = Acts 2:26) but is seized by the life-giving power of the Spirit. Christology reveals the central divergence from the Platonic teaching on spiritualization; its background is the theology of creation, whose inner unity is not destroyed but ratified by Christology.

But there is something more. As we have seen, the Christian liturgy linked up as a matter of historical necessity with the synagogue, not the Temple. In doing so it took on a more or less puritan form. Initially this was unavoidable, in order to express the fundamental gulf between it and the Old Law, which was focused in the Temple cult. If it was to be made clear that the Christian liturgy was not a mere multiplication of the Temple but a complete break leading to a new level, this break had to be consistently manifested in institutional terms. In fact, during the first decades of the Christian movement, the Temple and its ordinances still existed, and Jewish Christians continued to participate legitimately in its life; hence in any case there could be no question of imitating Temple worship. In spite of this we cannot avoid wondering how far such a central text as John 2:13–22, with its promise of a new Temple "in three days", affected the way Christianity saw itself and influenced it to take over the reality signified by the Temple.[23] This question is of great importance for the problem of the priestly office: does the primitive Church's connection solely with the synagogue, as a matter of necessity, imply a definitive and fundamental break with the idea of priesthood, or must the Temple's authentic inheritance be continued, once it has undergone a christo-logical transformation? This is only one of the instances which show plainly how intractable, so far, the problem of the relationship of the Testaments to one another has proved. Another instance is the question of the legitimacy of the church building, the "sacral" edifice—nowadays an increasingly pressing question. Then, out of this same melting pot, there comes the issue of images which has been so traumatic in Church history.

In fact, patristic theology did incorporate the idea of the Temple into Christianity; it was elevated to the level of a category in the understanding of the Christian reality.[24] For the most part, however, it was used "allegorically", in a strictly applied, spiritualizing theology; it was not until the iconoclastic controversy that the Greek

[23] On this, cf. the thorough study by Y. Congar, *The Mystery of the Temple* (London 1962). Valuable insights into the related question of the priesthood in A. Feuillet, *The Priesthood of Christ and His Ministers* (Doubleday 1975).

[24] Cf. my remarks in J. Ratzinger, *Volk und Haus Gottes in Augustins Lehre von der Kirche* (Munich 1954).

Church's passion for the image led to a breakthrough in which Christianity's historical development—with complete justification—succeeded in moving in the opposite direction: from the absence of images in the Old Testament to the glorification of God in the image.[25] This decision has been largely called into question in the postconciliar Catholic Church, and the only possible course, people have felt, is to abandon images. This results from the same approach which wants to remove "actual church music" from worship; it shows how close today's issues are to those of yesterday, once one penetrates below the surface.

The results are surprisingly similar. The idea that God can only really be praised in the heart means that no status can be accorded to music, to the audible form of this praise, within the act of praise itself in Christian worship. Yet, as a matter of fact, the worship of God *has* a vocal form; there *is* singing in worship. As a way of getting around this, music must be relegated to a secondary level. Augustine is a splendid example of this. His sensitivity to music caused him much torment because his mind was dominated by a spiritualizing theology which ascribed the senses to the Old Testament, the "old man", the old world: he is afraid of "sinning grievously" when he is "moved more by the music than by the reality to which the singing refers"—and would prefer "not to hear singing at all". Fortunately his rigorism is dampened when he recalls the profound stirring his soul experienced when he first heard church music in Milan, and although he does not risk a final decision, he

[25] Cf. P. Evdokimov, *L'art de l'icône. Théologie de la beauté* (Desclée 1970); C. Schönborn, *L'icône du Christ. Fondements théologiques* (Fribourg 1976); valuable too is S. Harkianakis, *Orthodoxe Kirche und Katholizismus* (Munich 1975), 75–88.

is "more inclined to value the use of singing in church: by means of the delight of the ears, the soul which is still weak is encouraged to rise to the world of piety".[26] Thomas was justified in seeing here a confirmation of Boethius' theory of music and could sum up his reasons for church music by saying that "thus the minds of the weak are more effectively summoned to piety".[27] So church music is put at the level of what is pedagogically useful; in practice, therefore, it is subject to the criterion of "utility".

We shall show that both Thomas and Augustine can go much further than this, in fact, on the basis of their experience and understanding. But the "spiritualization" framework which had become part of the question of the relation of the two Testaments (and hence of what is

---

[26] *Confessions* X, 33,50; Thomas, q 91 a 2 resp.

[27] Thomas, ibid.; cf. Boethius, *De institutione musica*, Prol. PL 63:1168. With a certain justification, Thomas supports his argument by reference to the eighth book of Aristotle's *Politics*, although he by no means exhausts the richness it contains. If one recalls that Aristotle devotes almost this entire eighth book to music, it becomes clear just how important a place he assigns to music in his philosophy of community. Among the four disciplines which according to Aristotle form the rootstock of education—writing (γράμματα), gymnastics, music and drawing (γραφική) (VIII 3, Bekker II 1337b, 24f.)—music is given a special place. Unlike the other three, it is not oriented to a trade and a purpose but instructs man in true leisure, which needs no extrinsic justification but has an intrinsic purpose: "ταύτας τὰς μαθήσεις ἑαυτῶν χάριν, τὰς δὲ πρὸς τὴν ἀσχολίαν . . . χάριν ἄλλων" (VIII 3; 1338a, 12f.). Cf. also the splendid verdict: "The lofty mind, the free man is not always asking what use a thing is" (1338b, 2ff.). In the philosophy of music of Aristotle's *Politics*, we become aware of a side of Greek thought which is largely forgotten, as H. I. Marrou emphasizes: "As we see the Greeks through the medium of our own classical culture, they seem to us to be primarily poets, philosophers and mathematicians; if we honor them as artists, we think of them primarily as

specifically Christian) stops them from carrying their insight through consistently.

b. First, however, we must bring to light a second group of ideas which stood in the way of a positive evaluation of church music. Only by understanding the reasons for the denial of church music can we show forth the positive rationale in a convincing manner. The matter is put in a nutshell in Thomas' fundamental article on the praise of God, where he says that "vocal worship is necessary, not for God's sake, but for the sake of the worshipper".[28] Here we see how much the ancient world's concept of God's absolute immutability and impassibility had entered into Christian thought through Greek philosophy, creating a barrier to any satisfactory theology, not only of church music, but of all prayer whatever. In Aristotle this concept of God had led logically to the identification of piety with self-culture,

---

architects and sculptors; as a result of our education we give less attention to their music than to their ceramics! Yet, in fact and in intention, they were musicians first and foremost." (*Geschichte der Erziehung im klassischen Altertum*, [Freiburg-Munich 1957], 68 [*Histoire de l'éducation dans l'antiquité* (Paris 1955); History of Education in Antiquity (London 1956)]). Certainly, Plato's purism (*Politeia* III 398a–400a) pursues a different line, which, in late classical times, could without difficulty be combined with the puritanism of the synagogue, cf. note 44. It is a pity that in this issue Thomas was inhibited by the patristic authorities and hence was not able to follow Aristotle's lead into a Christian context, with the result that, as yet, we have no "Christian Aristotle" in the theory of church music. Considering that, as far as the Christian is concerned, the Church, by virtue of her locus in the structure of existence, has taken over the place of the *polis* of the ancient world, the Aristotelian connection of *polis* and music could have yielded an ideal starting point in the question of church music. A brief summary of the form and development of Greek music can be found in *Der kleine Pauly* 3: 1485–96.

[28] Q 91 a 1 resp.

that is, the cultivation of what is most pleasing to the gods, namely, reason.[29] Only with great difficulty has Christian theology, dominated by the idea of immutability, been able to shake free from these notions; indeed, the regression today into a theory in which prayer is simply the activation of those of man's powers which are felt to be "the best" has assumed frightening proportions. No doubt classical theology is far removed from this kind of rationalism; liberated by Christ, who is the Word of God, it knows that it is enabled to speak with God; but in the philosophical superstructure the influence of the old ideas of God still makes itself felt; hence a shadow of rationalism is cast over the theory of liturgy.

3. The Theological Basis of Church Music

We have spoken of the commitment to the "spiritualization" framework, and to the ancient concept of God, as the burden of the theological tradition; on the other hand, the latter's freedom and breadth spring from two sources internal to Christianity: the living experience of liturgy and the theology of the psalms. With the transition from the synagogue to the church, singing in worship had increased; at a very early date "hymns" had been

[29] *Nichomach. Ethics* X 9 Bekker 1179a, 24ff. Cf. the commentary by F. Dirlmeier (*Aristoteles, Nikomachische Ethik*, Darmstadt 1956), 598f., where he shows that the philosophical achievement of this passage lies in the way it sublimates the *do ut des*, so that, in spite of the axiomatic self-love of the gods, Aristotle is able to present an impressive picture of the friendship with the gods enjoyed by the man of insight. On the problem of immutability in Christian theology, cf. W. Maas, *Unveränderlichkeit Gottes. Zum Verhältnis von griechisch-philosophischer und christlicher Gotteslehre* (Paderborn 1974). See also the first article in the present volume.

added to the psalms.[30] In contrast to theology, the psalms manifested an utterly unpuritanical delight in music, which, in spite of allegorical exegesis, was bound to have an influence. The fact that these songs of Israel continued to be prayed and sung as hymns of the Church meant that the whole wealth of feeling of Israel's prayer was present in the Church. Thus Thomas too concludes his reflections on the vocal quality of prayer with a quotation from the psalms which goes far beyond the considerations that precede it: ". . . his praise shall continually be in my mouth. . . . Let the afflicted hear and be glad. O magnify the Lord with me. . . ."[31] Here, delight in the Lord is felt to be meaningful and beautiful in itself; joy in shared praise of him, the awareness, through celebratory music-making, that God is worthy of worship—this is self-evident, it needs no theories. By quoting from the psalms, Thomas is in fact saying Yes to that joy which *expresses* itself and in doing so unites those who participate (and this includes particularly those who "listen"); this expressed joy manifests itself as the presence of the glory which is God: in responding to this glory, it actually *shares* in it. It would not be difficult to take this theme of "glorification", found in the Old Testament in the context of the theology of creation, and fill it out in

[30] Hymns of this kind are indicated in 1 Cor 14:25–26; Col 3:16; Eph 5:18ff. The New Testament contains quite a number of early Christian hymns, e.g., Phil 2:5ff.; Eph 2:14–16; 2 Tim 2:11–13. They are collected in H. Schlier, *Das Ende der Zeit* (Freiburg 1971), 212f.; cf. also S. Corbin, "Grundlagen und erste Entwicklung der christlichen Kultmusik", in Fellerer, *Geschichte*, 16–21. I have endeavored to show these connections in more detail in my article "Theologische Probleme der Kirchenmusik", in *Internat. kath. Zeitschrift* 9 (1980): 148–57.

[31] Ps 33:2–4; Thomas q 91 a 1 resp. Cf. also St. Thomas' commentary on Ps 33 (1–4), which develops these ideas a little further.

terms of Christology (Christ as the glory of God now accessible to us) and pneumatology (the Spirit speaks, sighs and gives thanks in us).[32] As opposed to a narrow, rationalistic theory of proclamation, we would need to point to that cosmic proclamation which finds expression in Psalm 19: the heavens are telling the glory of God. The Creator's glory cannot be manifested in word only: it needs to be expressed in the music of creation, too, and in its creative transformation by the mind of the believing and beholding man. At the same time we would need to remind ourselves that the psalms are also the prayers of the poor, the prayer of the crucified Righteous One, and as such they are to a large extent laments; but here too they are to be seen as the lament of the whole creation, which goes beyond words, transforming them into a music in which the lament becomes both a beseeching of God and a sign of hope: glory, too, but in the mode of suffering.

"Glorification" is the central reason why Christian liturgy must be cosmic liturgy, why it must as it were orchestrate the mystery of Christ with all the voices of creation.[33]

The other themes found in the tradition represented by Thomas can be fitted into this basic context and fill it

[32] The trinitarian dimension of church music is very well described in the important article by F. Haberl entitled "Zur Theologie der Kirchenmusik", in *Musica sacra* 91 (1971): 213–19; cf. id., "Die humane und sakrale Bedeutung der Musik", in H. Lonnendonker, *In caritate et veritate. Festschrift für Joh. Overath* (Saarbrücken 1973), 17–23.

[33] Cf. the magnificent outline of a theological aesthetics by H. U. von Balthasar, *Herrlichkeit*, 7 vols. (Einsiedeln 1967–69) [*The Glory of the Lord* (San Francisco: Ignatius, 1982-)]; id., *Kosmische Liturgie. Das Weltbild Maximus' des Bekenners*, 2nd ed. (Einsiedeln 1961).

out. Thus, for instance, Thomas says that through the
praise of God man ascends to God.[34] Praise itself is
a movement, a path; it is more than understanding,
knowing and doing—it is an "ascent", a way of reaching
him who dwells amid the praises of the angels. Thomas
mentioned another factor: this ascent draws man away
from what is opposed to God. Anyone who has ever
experienced the transforming power of great liturgy,
great art, great music, will know this. Thomas adds that
the sound of musical praise leads us and others to a sense
of reverence.[35] It awakens the inner man,[36] as Augustine
had discovered in Milan. With Augustine the academic,
a man who had come to appreciate Christianity as a
philosophy but was uneasy about the Church herself,
which seemed to have a lot of vulgarity about her, it
was the singing Church which gave him a shattering
experience, penetrating the whole man, and which led him
forward on the way to the Church.[37] From this point of

---

[34] . . . *homo per divinam laudem affectu ascendit in Deum*: q 91 a 1 resp.

[35] . . . *ut nos ipsos et alios audientes ad eius reverentiam inducamur*: ibid.

[36] *Valet tamen exterior laus oris ad excitandum interiorem affectum laudantis*: q 91 a 1 ad 2.

[37] Cf. the beautiful description in *Confessions* IX 6,14: "How I wept to hear Your hymns and songs, deeply moved by the voices of Your sweetly (suave) singing Church! Their voices penetrated my ears, and with them truth found its way into my heart; my frozen feeling for God began to thaw, tears flowed and I experienced joy and relief." On the idea of *suave* ("sweetly"), cf. E. Werner, in Fellerer, *Geschichte*, 26: the cantor was required to sing with a "sweet" voice, i.e., a high, lyrical voice of tenor quality. Augustine's other statements on church music do not match up, however, to this testimony to direct experience because of the influence of his theory of spiritualization. Apart from *Conf.* X 33,50, mention should be made of his *Epist.* 55 to Januarius. Here he says that, with regard to following the custom of the particular church, it is praiseworthy if she ministers to

view, the other, pedagogical aspect, the "stimulating of others to praise God",[38] becomes meaningful and intelligible, particularly when we recall what "pedagogy" meant for the ancients, namely, a leading to one's real nature, a process of redemption and liberation.[39]

---

the weakness of the little ones, a principle which is based on the use of hymns and psalms and spiritual songs, authorized by the Lord and the apostles. It is interesting that the Donatists criticized the musical puritanism of the African Catholics, which made many Catholics even more sceptical with regard to church music: XVIII, 34 *CSEL* 34,2 p. 208f. This leads us to conclude that the Donatist liturgy adopted large elements of indigenous musical tradition (which would correspond to the markedly African and nationalist quality of Donatism). Hence Augustine's reserve in the matter of church music may be traceable not only to his spiritualization philosophy but also to the Catholic-Donatist controversy. In *Enarr. II in Ps 18,1* (C.Chr XXXVIII, 105), Augustine distinguishes human singing from birdsong: the birds sing what they do not understand. "But we who have learned in the Church how to sing the divine words must recall what is written: blessed the people which sings praises with understanding. Therefore, my beloved, what we have sung with united voices we must understand and appreciate with perceptive hearts." On Augustine and the Milan liturgy, cf. B. Baroffio, in Fellerer, *Geschichte*, 192; on Augustine's path from intellectual to ecclesial Christianity, cf. F. van der Meer, *Augustinus der Seelsorger* (Cologne 1951), 25ff.; J. Ratzinger, *Volk und Haus Gottes in Augustins Lehre von der Kirche*, 1–12.

[38] Thomas q 91 a 1 ad 2: . . . *ad provocandum alios ad laudem Dei*.

[39] G. Greshake emphasized the religious depth of the concept of *paideia* in "Der Wandel der Erlösungsvorstellungen in der Theologiegeschichte", in L. Scheffczyk, *Erlösung und Emanzipation* (Freiburg 1973), 76ff. In fact the theory of music which Aristotle develops in book eight of the *Politics* is governed by the idea of *paideia*. In musical education *paideia* goes far beyond a training in what is useful and necessary: it facilitates authentic leisure and hence is an education for freedom, for beauty: ". . . ἐστὶ παιδεία τις ἥν οὐχ ὡς χρησίμην παιδρυτέον . . . ἀλλ' ὡς ἐλευθέριον καὶ καλήν" (VIII 3, Bekker 1338a, 30ff.).

4. The Positive Significance of the Theological Critique of Music

In undertaking to identify and develop the positive elements of the tradition, we must face the question of to what extent its critical stance may be justified. The very breadth of this aspect of the tradition, with the substantial reasons given (however qualified), oblige us to do so. We found that the basic reason underlying all particular criticisms is the idea of "spiritualization", which expresses the transition from the Old to the New Testament and hence the special orientation of Christianity. We discovered that this element is misunderstood if it is simply equated with the denial of the "senses", of man's bodily nature, and with the renunciation of the fullness of creation. The movement of spiritualization in creation is understood properly as bringing creation into the mode of being of the Holy Spirit and its consequent transformation, exemplified in the crucified and resurrected Christ. In this sense, the taking up of music into the liturgy must be its taking up into the Spirit, a transformation which implies both death and resurrection. That is why the Church has had to be critical of all ethnic music; it could not be allowed untransformed into the sanctuary. The cultic music of pagan religions has a different status in human existence from the music which glorifies God in creation. Through rhythm and melody themselves, pagan music often endeavors to elicit an ecstasy of the senses, but without elevating the senses into the spirit; on the contrary, it attempts to swallow up the spirit in the senses as a means of release. This imbalance toward the senses recurs in modern popular music: the "God" found here, the salvation of man identified here, is quite different from the God of the Christian faith. Quite different coordinates of existence are applied, quite a contrary view of the cosmos as a whole is exhibited. Here music can indeed become a "seduction" leading men astray. Here music does not purify but becomes a drug, an anesthetic. Superficially, the reason why elements of African pagan music are taken up with such facility into post-Christian pagan music may seem to have to do with a similarity of formal components; but the deeper reason lies in their basically sympathetic attitudes, their understanding of reality, for, at heart, the "enlightened" technological world can be both pagan and primitive. If music is to be the medium of worship, it needs purifying; only then can it in turn have a purifying and "elevating" effect.

The whole of Church history can be seen as the struggle to achieve the proper kind of spiritualization; and although, musically speaking, the theologians' puritanism was frequently unenlightened, the fruit of this struggle has been the great church music of the West—indeed, Western music as a whole. The work of a Palestrina or a Mozart would be unthinkable apart from this dramatic interplay in which creation becomes the instrument of the spirit, and the spirit, too, becomes organized sound in the material creation, thus attaining a height inaccessible to "pure" spirit. Spiritualization of the senses is the true spiritualization of the spirit. No one could have foreseen, at the outset of this process, the fruits it would yield. To that extent it is impossible to lay down a priori musical criteria for this spiritualization process, although it is certainly easier to say what is excluded than what is included. Vatican II was well advised, therefore, only to indicate very general standards:

music must "accord with the spirit of the liturgical
action";[40] it must be "suitable", or be capable of being
"made suitable, for sacred use";[41] it must "accord with
the dignity of the temple" and "truly contribute to the
edification of the faithful".[42]

At this point the tradition embodied by Thomas is
clearer. The text we have analyzed presents us with two
clear limits: following an apparently undisputed tradition,
he insists on the strictly vocal character of church music.
Behind Jerome's rasping criticisms we can see the bitter
dispute between the early Church and the ancient theatre
which exercised such a fascination; it is the music of the
theatre which Jerome wishes to exclude, not because
it exemplifies the ecstatic character of earlier cultic
music, but because of the vanity and affectation in
which it involves the artist concerned. Here we can
agree unreservedly with him: liturgical music must be
humble, for its aim is not applause but "edification".
It is appropriate that in church, unlike the concert hall,
the musician is for the most part not seen. But what shall
we say of the express option in favor of vocal music? It
should be clear from what we have already said that
Thomas' exclusive espousal of it is based historically and
in fact on a misunderstanding. All the same I would
hesitate to dismiss such a deeply rooted tradition as
completely mistaken. We must surely admit that the
liturgy of the incarnate Word is necessarily and specifically word-oriented. To say this is not to be a party to
the banal rationalism of the postconciliar period, which
held that only what everyone could follow intellectually

[40] Art. 116.
[41] Art. 120.
[42] Ibid.

was suitable for liturgy, a view which led to the exclusion of art and the increasingly banal treatment of the "word". These false conceptions are parried at the conclusion of Aquinas' *quaestio* on music: he is dealing with the objection that when something is sung it is harder for the hearers to understand than when it is said. He replies: "Even if those who listen sometimes do not understand the words being sung, they do understand the reason for the singing, namely, the praise of God. And that is sufficient to arouse men to worship."[43] A relation to the word, then, is fundamental all the same. Perhaps it should be said that, where an instrument is concerned, there is a greater possibility of alienation from the spirit than in the case of the voice; music can slip away from or turn against the spirit, the more remote it is from the human being. Conversely this would mean that, with instruments, the process of purification, of elevation to the spirit, must be considered with special care. But here again it is this essential purification which has resulted in the development of the instruments of Western music, endowing mankind with its most precious gifts. Man fails to measure up to this inheritance to the extent that he rejects the claim which the spirit of faith makes upon the senses. The struggle between faith and the world's music has been most fruitful.[44]

[43] Q 91 a 2 opp.5 and ad 5.

[44] A related debate can already be found in Aristotle, where he distinguishes Doric music as "ethical" music from the "orgiastic and pathetic" Phrygian music and excludes the latter from education (VIII 7, Bekker 1341f.); characteristically he adduces the myth of Athene's rejection of the flute: for him such music contradicts the spiritualized humanity symbolized in Athene (VIII 6, Bekker 1341b, 2ff.). Here we clearly see the continuing influence of ancient cultic and cultural

Conclusion: Governing Principles
In This Time of Crisis

To conclude these observations I would like to put forward a number of basic principles, applying what we have discovered from history to the current problems which formed our starting point.

1. Liturgy is for all. It must be "catholic", i.e., communicable to all the faithful without distinction of place, origin and education. Thus it must be "simple". But that is not the same as being cheap. There is a banal simplism, and there is the simplicity which is the expression of maturity. It is this second, true simplicity which applies in the Church. The greatest efforts of the spirit, the greatest purification, the greatest maturity—all these are needed to produce genuine simplicity. The requirement of simplicity, properly speaking, is identical with the requirement of purity and maturity. Certainly there are many stages on the way to it, but each one makes demands on the soul without which nothing is achieved.

---

oppositions. For Aristotle, Lydian music is suitable for education, however, because it combines a sense of beauty with an educative content (VIII 7, Bekker 1342b, 31f.). But, in his magnanimous and open approach, he allows Phrygian music for relief (catharsis). He deliberately adopts this tolerant attitude in opposition to Plato in the Politeia, who excluded Mixolydian, Hyperlydian ("syntonolydisti"), Ionic and Lydian music from his ideal state, only permitting Doric and Phrygian music; and as for instruments, Plato wanted to allow nothing but the lyre and cithara in the city, and a kind of reed-pipe in the country. Here too, behind the philosophical deduction one can perceive a mythico-religious substratum: "For we are doing nothing new . . . by giving the preeminence to Apollo and his instruments before Marsyas and his" (*Republic* III 399e, cf. III 398d–400a).

2. Catholicity does not mean uniformity. Vatican II had a purpose in making special mention of the cathedral church in its Constitution on the Liturgy. The cathedral can and should be more ambitious than the normal parish church in terms of the solemnity and beauty of the worship of God, and here too art will be involved at different levels depending on the occasion and the prevailing conditions. Together we make up the whole; we do not all have to be doing everything. It is strange that the postconciliar pluralism has created uniformity in one respect at least: it will not tolerate a high standard of expression. We need to counter this by reinstating the whole range of possibilities within the unity of the Catholic liturgy.

3. One of the principles of the Council's liturgical reform was, with good reason, the *participatio actuosa*, the active participation of the whole "People of God" in the liturgy. Subsequently, however, this idea has been fatally narrowed down, giving the impression that active participation is only present where there is evidence of external activity—speaking, singing, preaching, liturgical action. It may be that articles 28 and 30 of the Constitution on the Liturgy, which define active participation, have encouraged this narrow view by speaking largely of external activities. Yet article 30 also speaks of silence as a mode of active participation. We must go on to say that listening, the receptive employment of the senses and the mind, spiritual participation, are surely just as much "activity" as speaking is. Are receptivity, perception, being moved, not "active" things too? What we have here, surely, is a diminished view of man which reduces him to what is verbally intelligible, and this at a time when we are aware that what comes to the surface in

rationality is only the tip of the iceberg compared with the totality of man. In more concrete terms, there are a good number of people who can sing better "with the heart" than "with the mouth"; but their hearts are really stimulated to sing through the singing of those who *have* the gift of singing "with their mouths". It is as if they themselves actually sing in the others; their thankful listening is united with the voices of the singers in the one worship of God. Are we to compel people to sing when they cannot, and, by doing so, silence not only their hearts but the hearts of others too? This is not to impugn the singing of the whole faithful people, which has its inalienable place in the Church, but it *is* opposed to a one-sidedness which is founded neither on tradition nor on the nature of the case.

4. A Church which only makes use of "utility" music has fallen for what is, in fact, useless. She too becomes ineffectual. For her mission is a far higher one. As the Old Testament speaks of the Temple, the Church is to be the place of "glory", and as such, too, the place where mankind's cry of distress is brought to the ear of God. The Church must not settle down with what is merely comfortable and serviceable at the parish level; she must arouse the voice of the cosmos and, by glorifying the Creator, elicit the glory of the cosmos itself, making it also glorious, beautiful, habitable and beloved. Next to the saints, the art which the Church has produced is the only real "apologia" for her history. It is this glory which witnesses to the Lord, not theology's clever explanations for all the terrible things which, lamentably, fill the pages of her history. The Church is to transform, improve, "humanize" the world—but how can she do that if at the same time she turns her back on beauty, which is so closely allied to love? For

together, beauty and love form the true consolation in this world, bringing it as near as possible to the world of the resurrection. The Church must maintain high standards; she must be a place where beauty can be at home; she must lead the struggle for that "spiritualization" without which the world becomes the "first circle of hell". Thus to ask what is "suitable" must always be the same as asking what is "worthy"; it must constantly challenge us to seek what is "worthy" of the Church's worship.

5. The Constitution on the Liturgy observes that "in certain countries, especially in mission lands, there are people who have their own musical tradition, and this plays a great part in their religious and social life. For this reason their music should be held in proper esteem and a suitable place is to be given to it."[45] This corresponds to the Council's idea of catholicity, according to which "whatever goodness is found in the minds and hearts of men, or in the particular customs and cultures of peoples, far from being lost is purified, raised to a higher level and reaches its perfection. . . ."[46] These expressions have been rightly welcomed in theology and pastoral care, even if on occasion the element of "purification" has been neglected. It is strange however that, in their legitimate delight in the new openness to other cultures, many people seem to have forgotten that the countries of Europe also have a musical inheritance which "plays a great part in their religious and social life"! Indeed, here we have a musical tradition which has sprung from the very heart of the Church and her faith. One cannot, of course, simply equate the great treasury of European

[45] Art. 119.
[46] *Ad gentes*, I 9.

church music with the music of the Church, nor, on account of its stature, consider that its history has come to an end; it would be equally impossible simply to identify the great figures of Latin theology with the teaching of the Church or to see in them some ultimate theological perfection. All the same it is just as clear that the Church must not lose this rich inheritance which was developed in her own matrix and yet belongs to the whole of humanity.[47] Or does this "esteem" and a "suitable place" in the liturgy (art. 119) apply only to non-Christian tradition? Fortunately the Council itself clearly opposes any such absurd conclusion, insisting that "the treasury of sacred music is to be preserved and cultivated with great care" (art. 114). Music such as this can only be preserved and cultivated, however, if it continues to be sung and played as prayer, as a gesture glorifying God, in the place where it was born—in the Church's worship.

---

[47] F. Haberl puts it splendidly in "Zur Theologie der Kirchenmusik", loc. cit., 218: "Church music must be both a traditional and a progressive art". On this whole issue, cf. also the valuable contribution by J. F. Doppelbauer, "Kompositorische Fragen und Aufgaben", in J. Overath, *Magna gloria Domini* (Altötting 1972), 148–56, where, from a musical point of view, he arrives at the same conclusions as we have reached through examining the theological sources.

What Corpus Christi Means to Me

Three Meditations

I

What does Corpus Christi mean to me? Well, first of all it brings back memories of special feast days when we took quite literally what Thomas Aquinas put so well in one of his Corpus Christi hymns: *Quantum potes tantum aude*—dare to do as much as you can, giving him due praise. . . . In fact these words also recall something Justin Martyr said as early as the second century. In his description of the Christian liturgy he writes that the one who presides at the eucharistic celebration, i.e., the priest, is to offer up prayers and thanksgivings "as much as he is able".[1] This is what the entire community feels called to do at Corpus Christi: dare to do what you can. I can still smell those carpets of flowers and the freshness of the birch trees; I can see all the houses decorated, the banners, the singing; I can still hear the village band, which indeed sometimes dared more, on this occasion, than it was able! I remember the *joie de vivre* of the local lads, firing their gun salutes—which was their way of welcoming Christ as a head of state, as *the* Head of State, the Lord of the world, present on their streets and in their village. On this day people celebrated the perpetual presence of Christ as if it were a state visit in which not even the smallest village was neglected.

[1] *Apol.* I 67,5.

Corpus Christi also brings to mind the issues raised by
the liturgical renewal with all its theological insights. Is it
right, we had to ask ourselves, to have this annual
celebration of the Eucharist in the form of a state visit of
the Lord of the world, with all the outward signs of
triumphal joy? We were reminded that the Eucharist was
instituted in the upper room—and somehow this must
be a normative factor. The signs of bread and wine,
chosen deliberately by the Lord, show that the Eucharist
is meant to be received as food. Therefore the correct
way of showing gratitude for the institution of the
sacrament is actually to celebrate the Eucharist; here we
celebrate his death and Resurrection and are built up by
him into the living Church. Anything else seemed to be a
misunderstanding of the Eucharist. Then we had a horror
of everything that looked like triumphalism: it seemed
irreconcilable with the Christian awareness of sin and
with the tragic situation of the world. So it was that
Corpus Christi became an embarrassment. The standard
textbook on liturgy which appeared between 1963 and
1965 does not even refer to Corpus Christi in its treatment
of the Church's year. Somewhat shamefacedly it offers
us a page under the heading "Eucharistic Devotions";
in its embarrassment it makes the curious suggestion that
the Corpus Christi procession should conclude with
communion of the sick, this being the only functional
rationale for a procession with the Host.[2]

The Council of Trent had been far less inhibited. It
said that the purpose of Corpus Christi was to arouse
gratitude in the hearts of men and to remind them of

[2] A. G. Martimort (ed.), *The Church at Prayer*, 2 vols. (New York
1968 and 1973).

their common Lord.[3] Here, in a nutshell, we have in fact three purposes: Corpus Christi is to counter man's forgetfulness, to elicit his thankfulness, and it has something to do with fellowship, with that unifying power which is at work where people are looking to the one Lord. A great deal could be said about this; for with our computers, meetings and appointments we have become appallingly thoughtless and forgetful.

Psychologists tell us that our rational, everyday consciousness is only the surface of what makes up the totality of our soul. But we are so hounded by this surface awareness that what lies in the depths can no longer find expression. Ultimately man becomes sick for sheer lack of authenticity; he no longer lives as a subject: he exists as the plaything of chance and superficiality. This is connected with our relationship to time. Our relationship to time is marked by forgetting. We live for the moment. We actually *want* to forget, for we do not want to face old age and death. But in reality this desire for oblivion is a lie: suddenly it changes into the aggressive demand for the future, as a way of destroying time. However, this romanticism of the future, this refusal to submit to time, is also a lie, a lie which destroys both man and the world. The only way to master time, in fact, is the way of forgiveness and thankfulness whereby we receive time as a gift and, in a spirit of gratitude, transform it.

[3] "Aequissimum est enim, sacros aliquos statutos esse dies, cum Christiani omnes singulari ac rara quadam significatione gratos et memores testentur animos erga communem Dominum et Redemptorem pro tam ineffabili et plane divino beneficio, quo mortis eius victoria et triumphus repraesentatur." Decr. de sc. Eucharistia (Sessio XIII, 11.10.1551) cap. 5; DS 1644.

Let us consider Trent again for a moment. There we find the unqualified statement that Corpus Christi celebrates Christ's triumph, his victory over death. Just as, according to our Bavarian custom, Christ was honored in the terms of a great state visit, Trent harks back to the practice of the ancient Romans who honored their victorious generals by holding triumphal processions on their return. The purpose of Christ's campaign was to eliminate death, that death which devours time and makes us cultivate the lie in order to forget or "kill" time. Nothing can make man laugh unless there is an answer to the question of death. And conversely, if there *is* an answer to death, it will make genuine joy possible—and joy is the basis for every feast. At its very heart the Eucharist is the answer to the question of death, for it is the encounter with that love which is stronger than death. Corpus Christi is the response to this central eucharistic mystery. Once a year it gives demonstrative expression to the triumphal joy in Christ's victory, as we accompany the Victor on his triumphal procession through the streets. So, far from detracting from the primacy of reception which is expressed in the gifts of bread and wine, it actually reveals fully and for the first time what "receiving" really means, namely, giving the Lord the reception due to the Victor. To receive him means to worship him; to receive him means, precisely, *Quantum potes tantum aude*—dare to do as much as you can.

The Council of Trent concludes its remarks on Corpus Christi with something which offends our ecumenical ears and has doubtless contributed not a little toward discrediting this feast in the opinion of our Protestant brethren. But if we purge its formulation of the passionate tone of the sixteenth century, we shall be surprised by something great and positive. First of all let us simply

listen to what Trent says. Corpus Christi must show
forth the triumph of the truth in such a way that, "in the
face of such magnificence and such joy on the part of the
whole Church, the enemies of the truth will either fade
away or, stricken with shame, attain to insight."[4] If we
remove the polemical element, what we have left is this:
the power in virtue of which truth carries the day can be
none other than *its own joy*. Unity does not come about
by polemics nor by academic argument but by the radiance
of Easter joy; this is what leads to the core of the
Christian profession, namely: Jesus is risen. This leads,
too, to the core of our humanity, which yearns for this
joy with its every fiber. So it is this Easter joy which is
fundamental to all ecumenical and missionary activity;
this is where Christians should vie with each other; this is
what they should show forth to the world. This too is
the purpose of Corpus Christi. In its deepest sense what
our dictum means (*quantum potes tantum aude*) is this: let
beauty shine out in all its radiance when you come to
express this joy of all joys. Love is stronger than death; in
Jesus Christ God is among us.

II

When we think of Corpus Christi, we think first of all of
the procession which marks this day. When the feast was
instituted in 1246, there was no procession. It is first
attested in Cologne in 1277, and nine years later it is also
found in Benediktbeuren. Since the fourteenth century,
therefore, it has been a permanent part of the day's

---

[4] ". . . ut eius adversarii, in conspectu tanti splendoris et in tanta
Ecclesiae laetitia positi, vel debilitati et fracti tabescant, vel pudore
affecti et confusi aliquando resipiscant." Ibid.

celebration on German soil; indeed, the procession has become a feature of the feast. But after Trent it was precisely the *procession* that presented difficulties. Why—so people said—carry the Host around? People could only imagine one meaningful kind of procession, a procession or pilgrimage *from* a place or places *to* a common celebration of the Eucharist somewhere else, i.e., a procession *to* the Eucharist, not *with* it. This is to exclude what is specific to the Corpus Christi procession. Behind this approach lay the idea that the only authentic liturgy was the old Roman liturgy, developed in the area of Rome in the first centuries. What had arisen in the Middle Ages and north of the Alps could only be regarded as the result of decadence and ignorance. Nowadays we have to learn all over again that the Church is always alive, in every period, and that therefore her development cannot be thought complete at any particular time, as if thereafter nothing of original value could be produced. Of course a preeminence attaches to the period of the founding of Christianity, when the permanent marks of its identity were being established. But the inner wealth contained in this identity was not exhausted then; it can develop and prove to be fruitful through all centuries.

How then are we to understand the Corpus Christi procession? I have found it helpful to take a look at its roots. First of all there is a general human factor which has caused processions to arise in all religious circles. Our relationship to God needs not only the inward aspect; it also needs to be expressed. And as well as speech, singing and silence, standing, sitting and kneeling, expression also calls for this celebratory walking along together in the community of the faithful, together with the God in whom we believe. In the Christian liturgy itself we can identify two elements which gave rise to the

Corpus Christi procession.[5] The liturgy of the "Great Week", in which the Church reenacts the drama of the last week of Jesus' life, presents two "processional" paths found in the sacred events themselves, namely, the procession of palms and Jesus' ascent to the Mount of Olives after the institution of the Eucharist. In the one he enters the Holy City in triumph; in the other he goes from it in prayer, into the darkness of night, into betrayal and death. There is a close relationship between these two processions: Jesus enters the city to cleanse the Temple, symbolically destroying it and thus incurring his death. This in turn is the inner precondition for his giving of himself in instituting the Eucharist and thus opening the new Temple of his love. Again, in sharing himself in the Eucharist, he is anticipating his death and looking forward to the Resurrection. But his departure from the city into the Passover night is a departure from the peaceful and protected sphere of salvation into the realm of death.[6] Very early on, the liturgy began to enact these processions in a solemn manner. In certain parts of France in the eleventh century the Blessed Sacrament was carried along in the procession of palms: it was a case of going beyond mere historical remembrance and of accompanying *Christus Victor* on his triumphal entry into his house to take possession of it once again. Essentially, the Holy Thursday procession is an accompanying of the Host, a walking with the Lord as he goes to deliver himself up for us. All this must be peripheral in Holy Week, but Corpus Christi brings these partial elements

[5] Cf. J. Pascher, *Das liturgische Jahr* (Munich 1963), 269ff.

[6] H. Gese, *Zur biblischen Theologie* (Munich 1977), 111, where this leaving behind of "the houses of Jerusalem, the only area of salvation and protection against . . . all evil" is interpreted against the background of the Passover tradition.

of the Easter mystery into the center and makes them into a special great feast. What was ambivalent on Palm Sunday, overshadowed by the darkness of the Cross, takes place publicly and on a grand scale at Corpus Christi in the joy of the Resurrection; the triumphal procession of the Lord, whom we publicly recognize as Lord, inviting him to take possession of our streets and squares.

There is a second root, namely, the "rogation" processions. We can see this connection in the custom [in Bavaria] of having four altars, from which in former times the four Gospels were sung. Throughout the whole history of religion, and thus here too, the number four symbolizes the four corners of the earth, i.e., the whole universe, the world in which we live. The blessing was imparted in four directions, with the intention of putting them under the protection of the eucharistic Lord. The four Gospels express the same thing. For they are inspired, they are the breath of the Holy Spirit, and their fourfold number expresses the world-embracing power of God's word and God's Spirit. The beginning of the Gospel stands for the whole; uttering it, one is as it were sending out the breath of the Holy Spirit to engage the four winds, pervading them and turning them to good. The world is thus declared to be the realm of God's creative word; matter is subordinated to the power of his Spirit. For matter too is his creation and hence the sphere of his gracious power. Ultimately we receive the very bread of the earth from his hands. How beautifully the new eucharistic bread is thus related to our daily bread! The eucharistic bread imparts its blessing to the daily bread, and each loaf of the latter silently points to him who wished to be the bread of us all. So the liturgy opens out into everyday life, into our earthly life and cares; it goes beyond the church precincts because it actually embraces heaven and earth, present and future. How we need this sign! Liturgy is not the private hobby of a particular group; it is about the bond which holds heaven and earth together, it is about the human race and the entire created world. In the Corpus Christi procession, faith's link with the earth, with the whole of reality, is represented "in bodily form", by the act of walking, of treading the ground, our ground; Joseph Pascher puts it well when he observes that this treading of the ground is related to the simple and eloquent rite of the imposition of hands.[7] The difference is that on this day we do not lay *our* hands on the earth, hands that so often exploit and violate it: we carry the Lord himself, the Creator, over the ground—the Lord who willed to give himself in the grain of the wheat and the fruit of the vine. So there is no contradiction between the rogation procession and the procession with the Blessed Sacrament which developed out of the liturgy of Holy Week; they come together on Corpus Christi in a single solemn profession of faith in the world-embracing power of Jesus Christ's redeeming love. Therefore when we walk our streets with the Lord on Corpus Christi, we do not need to look anxiously over our shoulders at our theological theories to see if everything is in order and can be accounted for, but we can open ourselves wide to the joy of the redeemed: *sacris sollemniis iuncta sint gaudia*— in joy let us celebrate the holy feasts.

[7] Op. cit., 286.

III

What does Corpus Christi mean to me? It does not only bring the liturgy to mind; for me, it is a day on which heaven and earth work together. In my mind's eye it is the time when spring is turning into summer; the sun is high in the sky, and crops are ripening in field and meadow. The Church's feasts make present the mystery of Christ, but Jesus Christ was immersed in the faith of the people of Israel and so, arising from this background in Israel's life, the Christian feasts are also involved with the rhythm of the year, the rhythm of seedtime and harvest. How could it be otherwise in a liturgy which has at its center the sign of bread, fruit of earth and heaven? Here this fruit of the earth, bread, is privileged to be the bearer of him in whom heaven and earth, God and man have become one. The way the Church's feasts fit in with the seasons of the year is therefore not an accident. Consequently we must go on to discover the inner rhythm of the Church's year and see the place Corpus Christi has within it.

First of all, clearly, it grows out of the mystery of Easter and Pentecost: it presupposes the Resurrection and the sending of the Spirit. But it is also in close proximity to the Feast of the Trinity, which reveals the inner logic in the connection between Easter and Pentecost. It is only because God himself is the eternal dialogue of love that he can speak and be spoken to. Only because he himself is relationship can we relate to him; only because he is love can he love and be loved in return. Only because he is threefold can he be the grain of wheat which dies and the bread of eternal life. Ultimately, then, Corpus Christi is an expression of faith in God, in love, in the fact that God is love. All that is said and done on Corpus Christi is in fact a single variation on the theme of love, what it is and what it does. In one of his Corpus Christi hymns Thomas Aquinas puts it beautifully: *nec sumptus consumitur*—love does not consume: it gives and, in giving, receives. And in giving it is not used up but renews itself. Since Corpus Christi is a confession of faith in love, it is totally appropriate that the day should focus on the mystery of transubstantiation. Love is transubstantiation, transformation. Corpus Christi tells us: Yes, there is such a thing as love, and therefore there is transformation, therefore there is hope. And hope gives us the strength to live and face the world. Perhaps it was good to have experienced doubts about the meaning of celebrating Corpus Christi, for it has led us to the rediscovery of a feast which, today, we need more than ever.

Eastward- or Westward-Facing Position?
A Correction

Nowadays the question of eastward- or westward-facing position is hardly mentioned any more. Nor would it be right, after the upheavals of past years, to press for further external changes. Therefore it seems all the more important to promote the kind of liturgical education which will enable people to participate in a proper inward manner, involving them in that movement, that direction, which is of the essence of the Eucharist. In doing so we must be aware of the mistaken approaches which can easily arise out of a misunderstanding of the liturgical reform.

In an impressive article in the International Catholic Review *Communio* 5, no. 4 (1978): 326–43, Everett A. Diederich spoke of "The Unfolding Presence of Christ in the Celebration of Mass", giving a sensitive treatment of the liturgy's inner dynamism as it proceeds step by step to make Christ present. Apropos he observed that in the old rite the Mass was celebrated facing the altar, that is, toward the holy of holies, an observation which caused me to make the following correction:

The eastward-facing position of the celebrant in the old Mass was never intended as a celebration toward the holy of holies, nor can it really be described as "facing the altar". In fact it would be contrary to all theological reason, since the Lord is present in the eucharistic gifts during the Mass in the same way as he is in the gifts of the tabernacle which come from the Mass. Thus the Eucharist would be celebrated "from" the Host "to" the Host, which is plainly meaningless. There is only one inner direction of the Eucharist, namely, from Christ in the Holy Spirit to the Father. The only question is how this can be best expressed in liturgical form.

Thus the positive content of the old eastward-facing direction lay not in its orientation to the tabernacle. It was twofold. The original meaning of what nowadays is called "the priest turning his back on the people" is, in fact—as J. A. Jungmann has consistently shown—the priest and people together facing the same way[1] in a common act of trinitarian worship, such as Augustine introduced, following the sermon, by the prayer *"Conversi ad Dominum"*. Priest and people were united in facing eastward; that is, a cosmic symbolism was drawn into the community celebration—a factor of considerable importance. For the true location and the true context of the eucharistic celebration is the whole cosmos. "Facing east" makes this cosmic dimension of the Eucharist present through liturgical gesture. Because of the rising sun, the east—*oriens*—was naturally both a symbol of the Resurrection (and to that extent it was not merely a christological statement but also a reminder of the Father's power and the influence of the Holy Spirit) and a presentation of the hope of the parousia. Where priest and people together face the same way, what we have is a cosmic orientation and also an interpretation of the Eucharist in terms of resurrection and trinitarian theology. Hence it is also an interpretation in terms of parousia, a theology of hope, in which every Mass is an approach to

[1] Cf. the review by J. A. Jungmann of O. Nussbaum's work *Der Standort des Liturgen am christlichen Altar vor dem Jahre 1000*, 2 vols. (Bonn 1965), in *ZKTh* 88 (1966): 445–50.

the return of Christ. In short, what Fr. Diederich calls "facing the altar" was in reality expressing a view of the eucharistic celebration in the context of cosmos and parousia.

It must be added that, according to E. Peterson,[2] this eastward-facing position for prayer, making the cosmos a sign of Christ and thus defining the cosmos as the locus of prayer, was underlined very early on by the custom of placing a cross on the east wall of Christian meeting-houses. First this was seen as a sign of the returning Christ; later it became more and more a reminder of the Lord's historical Passion, and finally the eschatological idea disappeared almost entirely from the image of the cross. This primitive Christian tradition is behind the old rubric which ordered that there must be a cross on the altar. So what has come down to us in the altar cross is a relic of the ancient eastward orientation. It maintained the ancient tradition of praying to the Lord who is to come under the sign of the cross, a tradition with strong associations, in former times, with the cosmic symbol of the "east". So, with regard to the eastward-facing position of the celebration prior to the Council, one cannot talk of celebrating "toward" the altar, let alone "toward the holy of holies", but it can be said that the Mass was celebrated facing the image of the cross, which embodied in itself the whole theology of the *oriens*. In this sense

[2] E. Peterson, "Die geschichtliche Bedeutung Roman der jüdischen Gebetsrichtung", in id., *Frühkirche, Judentum und Gnosis* (Freiburg 1959), 1–14; id., "Das Kreuz und die Gebetsrichtung nach Osten", ibid., 15–35. For the development of the image of the cross, cf. E. Dinkler, *Signum crucis. Aufsätze zum Neuen Testament und zur christlichen Archäologie* (Tübingen 1967); id., *Das Apsismosaik von S. Apollinare in Classe* (Opladen 1964); P. Stockmeier, *Theologie und Kult des Kreuzes bei Joh. Chrysostomos* (Munich 1966).

there was a continuity going right back to the threshold of the apostolic era.

Now it must be admitted that, at least since the nineteenth century, not only had the awareness of the liturgy's cosmic orientation been lost, but there was also little understanding of the significance of the image of the cross as a point of reference for the Christian liturgy. Hence the ancient eastward orientation of the celebration became meaningless, and people could begin to speak of the priest celebrating "facing the wall" or imagine that he was celebrating toward the tabernacle. This misunderstanding alone can explain the sweeping triumph of the new celebration facing the people, a change which has taken place with amazing unanimity and speed, without any mandate (and perhaps for that very reason!). All this would be inconceivable if it had not been preceded by a prior loss of meaning from within.

The best results of liturgical scholarship, such as Fr. Diederich's article, explain the new orientation by referring to the inner dynamism of the liturgical action, as the community's progressive approach to the Lord. In this way the attempt is made to fuse the present direction of the celebration with the nature of the ancient Christian inheritance. Generally, however, this view is not shared by many people. The general view is totally determined by the strongly felt community character of the eucharistic celebration, in which priest and people face each other in a dialogue relationship. This does express *one* aspect of the Eucharist. But the danger is that it can make the congregation into a closed circle which is no longer aware of the explosive trinitarian dynamism which gives the Eucharist its greatness. A truly liturgical education will have to use all its resources to counter this idea of an autonomous, complacent community. The community does not carry on a dialogue with itself; it is engaged on a common journey toward the returning Lord. Here are three suggestions for this kind of education:

1. Today we are in the midst of a crisis in the anthropocentric view of the world, a crisis which pervades the whole of man's self-made world. At such a time we need to rediscover (and indeed we are rediscovering) the significance of creation. We also need to be reminded that liturgy involves the cosmos—that Christian liturgy is cosmic liturgy. In it we pray and sing in concert with everything "in heaven and earth and under the earth" (Phil 2:10), we join in with the praise rendered by the sun and the stars. Thus in church architecture, for instance, we should see to it that churches are not designed merely with human utility in mind, but that they stand in the cosmos, inviting the sun to be a sign of the praise of God and a sign of the mystery of Christ for the assembled community. A rediscovery of the value of the church building's eastward orientation would help, it seems to me, in recovering a spirituality which embraces the dimension of creation.

2. Traditionally, the "east" and the image of the cross (i.e., the cosmic and the soteriological aspects of spirituality) were fused; the cross itself, which may originally have had a purely eschatological significance, called to mind the Lord's suffering, faith in the Resurrection and the hope of the parousia, i.e., it signified the whole tension of the Christian concept of time. It is this tension which has transformed star time into human time and into God's time—for God *is not* time, but he *has* time for us. In so many ways the cross embodies the theology of the icon, which is a theology of incarnation and transfiguration; as against the proscription of images in the Old Testament (and in Islam), it indicates a new feature

in the view of God as a result of the Son's Incarnation:
God presents himself to our senses. Now, in the man
who is his Son, he is depictable.[3] There are many reasons
for the loss of the image which has occurred in the wake
of the Council, but it is not something we can accept
with equanimity. Surely we must regard it as a priority
to reestablish the meaning of the image of the cross,
which has been a constant shaping factor on the whole
tradition of faith. Even now, when the priest faces the
people, the cross could be placed on the altar in such a
way that both priest and people can see it. At the
eucharistic prayer they should not look at one another;
together they ought to behold him, the Pierced Savior
(Zech 12:10; Rev 1:7).

3. It always impresses me that our Protestant brethren,
in transforming the medieval liturgical forms, have
achieved a real balance between, on the one hand, the
relationship of the community to its leader and, on the
other, their common relationship to the cross. Their
whole basic approach laid great weight on the community
character of worship and the interplay of leader and
congregation, whereas in the Catholic liturgy of former
times this only consisted in the priest's turning round for
a brief "*Dominus vobiscum*" or to invite the people to
pray. But when it is a question of praying together,
Protestants, people and leader, together turn to the
image of the Crucified. I think we should seriously try
to learn from this. When we pray it is not necessary,
indeed it is not even appropriate, to look at one another;
the same is true when we receive Holy Communion.
Local conditions will determine how best we can do

---

[3] Cf. C. von Schönborn, *L'icône du Christ. Fondements théologiques*
(Fribourg 1976).

justice to these points. In many cases our second suggestion may be a practical way forward. Even in St. Peter's in Rome, as a result of the exaggerated and misconceived idea of "celebrating facing the people", the altar cross has been removed from the center of the altar, so that it does not obstruct the view between celebrant and congregation. But the cross on the altar is not obstructing the view; it is a common point of reference. It is an open "iconostasis" which, far from hindering unity, actually facilitates it: it is the image which draws and unites the attention of everyone. I would even be so bold as to suggest that the cross on the altar is actually a necessary precondition for celebrating toward the people. It would help in clarifying the distinction between the liturgy of the word and the liturgy of the Eucharist. The first is concerned with proclamation and hence with a direct, face-to-face situation, whereas the second is a matter of all of us worshipping together in response to the call *"Conversi ad Dominum"*—"Let us turn to the Lord; let us be converted to the Lord!"[4]

---

[4] I would also like to mention the valuable remarks made by F. J. Nüss, in *Internat. kath. Zeitschrift* 8 (1979): 573–75, in response to my presentation of the issue. Then, despite the criticism which can be leveled against it, mention should be made of the relevant research of K. Gamber, e.g., *Gemeinsames Erbe, Liturgische Neubesinnung aus dem Geist der frühen Kirche* (Regensburg 1980), 82–89; *Liturgie und Kirchenbau. Studien zur Geschichte der Messfeier und des Gotteshauses in der Frühzeit* (Regensburg 1976); *Die Reform der römischen Liturgie. Vorgeschichte und Problematik* (Regensburg 1979), 46–52.

Worship in the Parish Communities Fifteen Years after the Council

A Sermon Delivered to the Bishops' Conference in Fulda

"Worship in the parish communities fifteen years after the Council"—this was the main topic of our conference here in Fulda at the grave of St. Boniface. What then is our liturgical life like today? In asking this question we are bound to have mixed feelings. On the one hand we are glad about the awakening of a new sense of common responsibility, a new experience of fellowship and of community participation in the eucharistic mystery; we rejoice in the new understanding which is abroad since the Church's liturgy has been brought from behind the veils of history to stand before us, fresh in its simplicity and greatness of stature. But on the other hand, we are aware of the strife and dissension which have arisen concerning the liturgy and within it; we shiver a little in the face of too much talk, too little silence and a lack of beauty; we are obliged to recall so much arbitrary action, which reduced the dignity of the Lord's institution to the level of something embarrassingly cobbled together. So we have cause for thanksgiving but also no less cause to examine our consciences, and to help us do so I would like to make a few suggestions in this evening hour.

My first consideration is this: our topic refers to worship in the parish communities. "Community" is

the new discovery of the post–conciliar period. We have
called to mind once more that Eucharist, in the language
of the ancient Church, was called, among other things,
synaxis, the "meeting together", the assembly. It draws
and binds men together, unites them, builds up community. Conversely, the community experiences Eucharist
as fulfillment, as the center of its life, something in
which it shares as a totality. All this is true, but we must
remember that the scope of *synaxis* is much wider than
the individual community. Behind it stand those words
from the Gospel of John: Jesus wanted to die for the
nation, and not only for the nation but "to gather into
one the children of God who are scattered abroad" (Jn
11:52). The assembly to which Jesus Christ calls us is the
assembly of all the children of God. The Lord does not
assemble the parish community in order to enclose it but
in order to open it up. The man who allows himself to be
"assembled" by the Lord has plunged into a river which
will always be taking him beyond the limits of his self at
any one time. To be with the Lord means to be willing,
with him, to seek all the children of God. It is a favorite
theme of our time that the Church is "wherever two or
three are gathered in my name", but the reverse is also
true: the community is only "with the Lord" and
"gathered in his name" provided it is entirely at one with
the Church, wholly part of the whole. That is why, however much it lives in the here and now, in a particular place,
seeking the consent of the local community, Christian
liturgy is essentially Catholic, that is, it proceeds from
the whole and leads back to it, it leads to unity with the
pope, the bishops and the faithful of all times and places.
The Catholic element is not something added on externally, a legislative restriction of the community's freedom,
but something from the Lord himself who seeks everyone
and seeks to bring them all together. Liturgy is not

"made" by the community; the community receives it from the whole, in the same way that it receives its own self, as community, from the whole. And it can only remain an ecclesial community by continually giving itself back in commitment to this whole. Two things are of immediate practical importance here: 1. The forms which are binding upon the whole Church, in which the whole Church shares, are not a kind of spoon-feeding of the local community; they are an expression of the authenticity and greatness of the liturgy. 2. Eucharist must never be allowed to be used to bolster up a community's self-affirmation or self-enclosure. Its genuineness and rightness are vindicated in those situations where not every erstwhile "parish community" can have its own priest and its own parish worship. Then we can see whether we are only looking for the Eucharist in our own community as a means of self-affirmation and togetherness or whether we are willing to be found by the Lord who opens us out and leads us beyond frontiers. Where parishes are opened up to one another, are received by one another, they are learning in a small way what catholicity means, namely, not priding oneself on one's own traditions but seeing, in the opening of the frontiers, a liberation into that great and wide realm for which the deepest yearnings of our souls are waiting.

There is something else: the Council reminded us most explicitly that the liturgy is, in the Church's language, *actio*, an action. Therefore it implies the *participatio actuosa*, the active participation of all the faithful. But here again the impression has been given, to a greater or lesser extent, that, if the liturgy is to be the work of the community, it must also be created by it; and, putting it crudely, this led to its being measured by its entertainment value. The idea was to make it as exciting as possible, shaking up the standoffish, the fringe members, and drawing them into community; but, strangely, what happened was that, as a result of all this, the liturgy actually lost its authentic inner vibrancy. For this does not arise from what *we* do but from the fact that something is being done here which all our concerted efforts cannot achieve. What has created the liturgy's special position, down the centuries, is the fact that in it a supreme authority is operative, an authority which no one can arrogate to himself. In the liturgy the absolutely Other takes place, the absolutely Other comes among us. In his commentary on the Song of Songs, that primally and profoundly human poem on the yearning and the tragic quality of love, Gregory of Nyssa describes man as the creature who wants to break out of the prison of finitude, out of the closed confines of his ego and of this entire world. And it is true: this world is too small for man, even if he can fly to the Moon, or one day perhaps to Mars. He yearns for the Other, the totally Other, that which is beyond his own reach. Behind this is the longing to conquer death. In all their celebrations, men have always searched for that life which is greater than death. Man's appetite for joy, the ultimate quest for which he wanders restlessly from place to place, only makes sense if it can face the question of death. Eucharist means that the Lord's Resurrection gives us this joy which no one else can. So it is not enough to describe the Eucharist as the community meal. It cost the Lord his life, and only at this price can we enjoy the gift of the Resurrection. Therefore the Eucharist does not stand or fall by its effect on our feelings. Feelings come to an end, and ultimately all entertainment becomes tedious—as we know only too well nowadays. What we need is the presence in our lives of what is real and permanent so that we can approach it. No external participation and creativity is of any use unless it is a participation in this inner reality, in the way of the Lord, in God himself. Its aim is to lead us to this breakthrough to God. This involves two further practical considerations: liturgy is not a matter of variety and change; it is concerned with an ever-deeper experience of something that is beyond change because it is the very answer that we are seeking. Secondly, liturgy is not only concerned with the conscious mind and with what can be immediately understood at the superficial level, like newspaper headlines. Liturgy addresses the human being in all his depth, which goes far beyond our everyday awareness; there are things we only understand with the heart; the mind can gradually grow in understanding the more we allow our heart to illuminate it.

I would like to mention a third aspect involved in the proper celebration of the Eucharist. It is one of the happy features of worship in the wake of the Council that more and more people participate fully in the Eucharist by receiving the body of the Lord, communicating with him and, in him, with the whole Church of God. Yet do we not feel a slight uneasiness at times in the face of an entire congregation coming to communion? Paul urgently insisted that the Corinthians should "discern" the Lord's body (1 Cor 11:29): is this still happening? Occasionally one has the feeling that "communion" is regarded as part of the ritual—that it goes on automatically and is simply an expression of the community's identity. We need to regain a much stronger awareness that the Eucharist does not lose all its meaning where people do not communicate. By going to Communion without "discernment", we fail to reach the heights of what is taking place in Communion; we reduce the Lord's gift to the level of everyday ordinariness and manipulation. The Eucharist is not a ritual meal; it is the shared prayer of the Church, in which the Lord prays together with us and gives us himself. Therefore it remains something great and precious, it remains a true gift, even when we cannot communicate. If we understood this better and hence had a more correct view of the Eucharist itself, many pastoral problems—the position of the divorced and remarried in the Church, for instance—would cease to be such a burden.

One final remark: when we speak of worship in the parish community, we immediately think exclusively of the Eucharist. But this very fact expresses the regrettable narrowing and impoverishment which have overtaken us in these latter years. The Eucharist is the heart and center of our worshipping life, but in order to be this center it must have a many-layered whole in which to live. Eucharist presupposes baptism; it presupposes continual recourse to the sacrament of penance. The Holy Father has emphasized this most strongly in his encyclical "*Redemptor Hominis*". The first element of the Good News, he stresses, was "Repent!" "The Christ who invites us to the eucharistic meal is always the same Christ who exhorts us to penance, continually saying 'Repent!' " (IV, 20) Where penance disappears, the Eucharist is no longer discerned and, as the Lord's Eucharist, is destroyed. But Eucharist also presupposes marriage and ordination, the social and the public structure of the Church. It presupposes personal prayer, family prayer and the paraliturgical prayer of the parish community. I would just like to mention two of the richest and deepest prayers of Christendom, prayers which are able to draw us again and again into the vast river of eucharistic prayer: the Stations of the Cross and the Rosary. One of the reasons why, nowadays, we are so discountenanced by the appeal of Asiatic or apparently Asiatic religious practices is that we have forgotten these forms of prayer. The Rosary does not call for intense conscious efforts which would render it impossible but invites us to enter into the rhythm of quiet, peaceably bringing us peace and giving a name to this quietness: Jesus, the blessed fruit of the womb of Mary. Mary, who cherished the living Word in the recollected quiet of her heart and thus was privileged to become the Mother of the incarnate Word, is the abiding pattern for all genuine worship, the Star which illuminates even a dark heaven and shows us the way. May she, the Mother of the Church, intercede for us so that we may be enabled to fulfill more and more the Church's highest task: the glorification of the living God, from whom comes mankind's salvation. Amen.